CTESIAS: ON INDIA

CTESIAS
ON INDIA

*and fragments of his
minor works*

Introduction, Translation and
Commentary by
ANDREW NICHOLS

Bristol Classical Press

First published in 2011 by
Bristol Classical Press
an imprint of
Bloomsbury Academic
Bloomsbury Publishing Plc
50 Beford Square,
London WC1B 3DP

CIP records for this book are available from the
British Library and the Library of Congress

ISBN 978-1-85399-742-6

Typeset by Ray Davies
Printed and bound in Great Britain by
CPI Antony Rowe, Chippenham and Eastbourne

www.bloomsburyacademic.com

Contents

Contents

Acknowledgments

This book began as part of a PhD Dissertation at the University of Florida under the direction of Konstantinos Kapparis, who painstakingly corrected the entire translation and offered numerous criticisms and suggestions for the commentary. I am greatly indebted to him for all of his support and encouragement.

Deborah Blake and the staff at Bristol Classical Press; the staff at the Blegen and Gennadius libraries at the American School of Classical Studies in Athens; the staff at the Indian Institute Library and the Bodleian Library at the University of Oxford; the staff at the British School of Archaeology in Athens; The Finnish Oriental Society; The Metropolitan Museum of Art; The Rare Book & Manuscript Library at the University of Illinois; Holger Funk; Annemarie Sykes; Tina Williams; Karelisa Hartigan; Andrea Sterk; Generosa Sangco-Jackson; Mrs. Hämeen-Anttila. I would especially like to thank Robert Wagman for meticulously reading several drafts and whose advice and support throughout this entire endeavour have proven invaluable. I would like to give special thanks to Professor Klaus Karttunen who graciously agreed to read the manuscript and whose numerous corrections and suggestions have helped greatly improve this work. Of course any mistakes remaining are entirely my own.

Finally, I would like to thank my family for all of their support, especially my wife Amy, to whom this work is dedicated.

Preface

Along with his *Persika*, Ctesias' *Indika* was a popular and highly influential work in antiquity. A doctor serving at the court of the Persian king Artaxerxes II, Ctesias had the rare opportunity for a Greek to meet travellers and visitors from the far eastern reaches of the Persian Empire, merchants from along the Silk Road and Indians from near the Indus Valley. The work that resulted from this experience was the first monograph ever written on India by a western author. For the first time western readers were introduced to such fantastic lore as the unicorn and the martichora, along with information on real life, albeit exotic, subjects such as the parrot and the art of falconry. Confirming pre-existing conceptions of what were considered to be the edges of the earth, more than any other work Ctesias' *Indika* helped shape the Greek view of India before the campaigns of Alexander.

Despite its popularity in antiquity, the work did not survive in its original form. It was preserved in the form of a summary by the Byzantine Patriarch Photius and in numerous quotations by later authors. Offered here for the first time in over a century is a full English translation and commentary on all the extent fragments of the *Indika*. Also included are the fragments of Ctesias' minor works, which have never been translated into English.

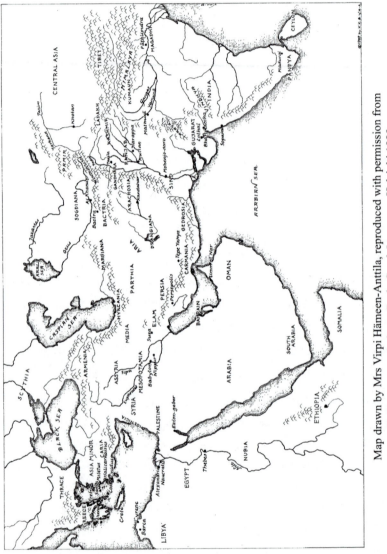

Map drawn by Mrs Virpi Hämeen-Anttila, reproduced with permission from
K. Karttunen, *India in Early Greek Literature*, Helsinki 1989.

Introduction

Ctesias of Cnidus was a medical doctor who lived in the latter half of the fifth and into the fourth century BCE. He served King Artaxerxes II of Persia as physician for the royal family until 398 BCE at which point he returned to Greece. In addition to several small treatises ranging from such topics as geography and medicine, he was the author of two major works on Eastern cultures with which he became familiar during his residency at the Persian court. The *Persika*, composed in 23 books, treats the history of the Persian Empire with the first six books dedicated to the Assyrian Empire to serve as an introduction. His other major work was the *Indika*, a monograph in one book on the ethnography of India, the earliest work on the region by a western writer of which there is any substantial knowledge.[1] Unfortunately, all of his works have been lost in their original form and have only been preserved in epitomes and quotations by later authors. These fragments, however, are substantial enough to provide a fairly clear notion of the nature and contents of the *Persika* and *Indika*.

The history of the text

Henricus Stephanus first published Photius' epitome of Ctesias along with epitomes of Memnon of Heraclea and Agatharchides of Cnidus in 1557. This same editor, wishing to compare the 'more reliable' Ctesias to Herodotus, added the epitome in an appendix to an edition of *The Histories* in 1566.[2] It was not until the nineteenth century that the first editions of all the fragments appeared, beginning with the text of Albert Lyon (1823), followed soon after by that of Johann Christian Felix Bähr (1824). The work of Bähr, which included a commentary and several new fragments, had a profound effect on the study of Ctesias for subsequent generations. In 1844 Carolus Müller produced a text accompanied by a Latin translation, which would mark the final appearance of the fragments of Ctesias as an appendix to *The Histories* of Herodotus. Müller took advantage of the editorial work produced in his time on many of the authors from whom the fragments of Ctesias are taken, most notably Bekker's critical edition of Photius.

The content of Ctesias' work covers a wide range of topics including Achaemenid Persian history, the western view of India before Alexander, and Greek history. By the late nineteenth century scholars began to pay attention to either the fragments of the *Persika* or the *Indika* individually rather than to the fragments as a whole. In 1881, John Watson McCrindle produced an English translation of the *Indika* with a commentary as part of a larger work on Greek authors who wrote about India and a few years later, John Gilmore edited a text of the *Persika* (1888), which were the first books to centre on an individual work of Ctesias, beginning a trend that would continue into the twentieth century. In 1947 Renée Henry's *Ctésias, la Perse, l'Inde, les sommaires de Photius* appeared with a French translation of Photius' epitome, which was republished in 1959 as part of his edition of the *Bibliotheca* of Photius, and in 1972 Friedrich Wilhelm König edited the *Persika*, accompanied by a German translation and commentary.

1958 marked the appearance of volume IIIC of Felix Jacoby's monumental *Die Fragmente der griechischen Historiker,* which contained all of the known fragments of Ctesias. It was the first complete collection of the fragments since Mueller's a century earlier and would last as the standard edition of Ctesias[3] until Dominique Lenfant's new text of 2004 with facing French translation. Lenfant retains Jacoby's numbering system but adds several new fragments to the corpus which were either omitted or overlooked by her predecessors. She takes a more conservative approach to textual criticism than Jacoby and her inclusion of the passages by Nicolaus of Damascus make for a fuller edition of the *Persika.*[4] Athena Hatzopoulou (2007) produced a text with Modern Greek translation and minimal commentary, however this work, which does not contain an *apparatus criticus*, is addressed to beginners and does not add much to the scholarship of Ctesias. Most recently, Jan Stronk (2010) has published a full text with English translation of the *Persika.* While I have consulted all of these editions, my translation is based for the most part on the text of Lenfant (and that of Jacoby when the latter includes a fuller passage).

Life of Ctesias

Not much is known of the life of Ctesias except what little can be gleaned from the fragments.[5] However, efforts have been made to reconstruct his biography with some success.[6] Ctesias was born sometime after the middle of the fifth century BCE in the city of Cnidus in Asia Minor[7] into a family of Asclepiads (F67) and studied medicine. He was the son of either Ctesiarchos or Ctesiochos (T1 and T1b; T11h), who was himself also probably a doctor as was his father before him (F68).

At some point towards the end of the fifth century he was brought to Persia to serve as physician for the royal family,[8] although it is unclear exactly when he arrived. According to Diodorus (T3 = F5 §32.4), Ctesias spent seventeen years at the Persian court. It is generally accepted that he left Persia in 398/397 BCE which would place his arrival at 415 BCE during the reign of Darius II. However, he is only referred to as the physician for Artaxerxes II and the detail given to the latter's reign in the *Persika* far exceeds that of Darius. This has lead some to consider that Ctesias actually spent seven years at the court rather than seventeen which would place his arrival in 405 BCE around the time of the ascendancy of Artaxerxes.[9]

While it is impossible to know for certain when and under what circumstances Ctesias came to Persia, his arrival during the reign of Darius cannot be excluded. He may well have arrived in 415 BCE, as the sources indicate, as a prisoner of war.[10] In any case, he was certainly in Persian service before the ascendancy of Artaxerxes, although he may have held no post of distinction until the latter's rise to power. There is no reason to assume that he immediately found a place of honour upon his arrival; but he may rather have simply been in the service of Darius tending to lesser members of the court.[11] He then would not have attained a distinguished position until the new king took the throne. He may even have been made the personal physician of Parysatis,[12] the wife of Darius, early on. While Parysatis seems to have exerted a powerful influence over Darius as she later would with her son,[13] as her physician Ctesias would not have had any special privileges other than acting as her confidant.

After his arrival in Persia, nothing is known of his stay until the Battle of Cunaxa (401 BCE) where serving as physician in the army of Artaxerxes II[14] he successfully treated the wound of the Great King. He remained close to the king during the battle, indicating that he already held the post of royal physician before 401 BCE. However, it was probably only after healing the king that Ctesias earned any real position of honour since there is no indication that doctors were viewed with distinction because of their practice. If he served Parysatis as her personal physician during the reign of Darius, it seems plausible that he regularly treated Artaxerxes himself as a child. The latter would then have been well familiar with Ctesias when he ascended the throne and so reasonably decided to employ a man he trusted as royal physician. This would also explain the statement of Diodorus that Ctesias served Artaxerxes for seventeen years, if one includes the years before the latter became king.

Soon after the battle, the Greek generals were imprisoned and executed, despite the support they received from Parysatis. Ctesias, as confidant of Parysatis and intermediary to the Greeks, assisted Clearchos by giving him a comb and arranging for a separate meal to be sent to the Greek general after his soldiers pilfered his food (F28). In return, Clearchos gave Ctesias his signet ring with dancing Caryatids depicted on it.[15] Since Ctesias no doubt did this at the behest of Parysatis, he found himself in the unusual position of earning the gratitude of both the king and the queen mother.[16]

Ctesias did, however, refuse to sneak Clearchos a dagger for suicide out of fear for his own personal safety. Certainly when one looks at the cruelty often displayed by members of the royal family towards their enemies, his fears seem justified. After all, during his tenure at the Persian court he witnessed (though probably not firsthand) the execution of all of the Greek generals by Artaxerxes and the cruel vengeance of Parysatis upon the enemies of her dead son Cyrus (F27). The most notable of these executions was that of Mithridates who was put to death in a most inhumane fashion, the trough-torture (F27 §16.3-7). Perhaps the most shocking deed of all was her assassination of the queen Stateira, an event that certainly would have lead Ctesias to the belief that no one at the court was safe. Under such circumstances, it is easy to see that he would welcome any opportunity to escape.

Fortunately for Ctesias, he would get his chance soon after the turn of the century when he took part as an intermediary in the communications between the king, Evagoras of Cyprian Salamis, and Conon of Athens, who had resided at the court of Evagoras since Aegospotamoi (T7c-d). Artaxerxes wished to check the power of the Spartans in the eastern Aegean,[17] which had grown considerably since the defeat of Athens in 404 BCE. Evagoras, meanwhile, who was a subject of the

Persian king, seems to have wanted to secure power over the whole of Cyprus where Spartan influence was strong and so proved to be a useful ally. He entered into negotiations with the king who made the most of the situation by employing the naval genius of Conon. Conon then entered into talks with the king through the intermediary of Ctesias who was ultimately charged with delivering two letters to Conon and the Spartans. The letter to the Spartans may have been sent in order to deceive them as to the king's own intentions.[18] In any case, Ctesias used this opportunity to return to his homeland of Cnidus where he composed his works on Persia and India.[19] These events, as Diodorus tells us (14.46), occurred in the second year of the 95th Olympiad thus firmly dating his return from Persia to the year 398/397 BCE.[20]

While we have no direct information on Ctesias' activities or travels within the empire, we can discern many of the places he likely visited.[21] He certainly would never be far from the royal family in case his services were needed. Thus we know he visited the capitals at Susa,[22] Ecbatana,[23] and possibly Persepolis were Artaxerxes was later buried,[24] all sites of major construction activity during the latter's reign. We also know then that Ctesias never visited India since there is no indication that Artaxerxes ever campaigned that far east. Conversely, he certainly visited Babylon,[25] possibly on more than one occasion, despite the fact that the king neglected this city in favour of the other capitals.[26] After the Battle of Cunaxa, Artaxerxes retired to Babylon (F27 §69) and there is no reason to believe that Ctesias did not accompany him.[27] Moreover, Ctesias assisted Clearchos while the Spartan general was imprisoned in Babylon soon after the battle[28] proving that Ctesias had visited the city.[29] It is also possible that he accompanied Parysatis to Babylon upon her brief exile after the assassination of Stateira since he was certainly closer to the queen mother than the king and obviously spent much more time in her attendance.

The *Indika*

The work for which Ctesias has been most maligned as an historian by ancients and moderns alike is his *Indika*. The work, which is the first full monograph on India, is filled with descriptions of fantastic beasts and monstrous peoples, causing many to discredit the work as of little historical value. However, the *Indika* is of extreme importance for the study of Greco-Persian views of India in the period before Alexander. Ctesias certainly never visited the country, but as a resident of the Persian court he had the unique opportunity, especially for a Greek, to encounter many travellers from India and the eastern edges of the known world. Since India was beyond the boarders of the Persian Empire and there is no indication that any Persian king campaigned beyond the Indus, the land was relatively unknown. India, like Ethiopia, was thought to be on the fringes of the world and inhabited by marvels and fanciful beings. Such places captured the imaginations of the Greeks and no doubt were of interest to the Persians as well.

The India of Ctesias' *Indika* refers only to the Indus valley and the sparsely populated northwest region the country. Like all Greeks and perhaps even Persians, he was unaware of the subcontinent. Hearing such stories of monstrous beings and flora with incredible properties would simply have reinforced Ctesias' typically Greek preconceived notions of the edge of the world. However, this certainly does not mean that he was simply creating stories from his own imagination, as has sometimes been argued.[30] He often related travellers' stories, many of which originated in the subcontinent,[31] and at times was able to view some of the animals or artifacts firsthand (see discussion below).

To be sure, there are many literary motifs in his *Indika* which are typical about peoples living on the edges of the world. Often sizes of flora and fauna are exceedingly large (e.g. the Indian reed and roosters) or small (e.g. Pygmies), sometimes only in regard to one feature (e.g. the unusually large ears of the Enotokoitai). The Indians were said to enjoy extreme longevity,[32] be very just in their customs,[33] and inhabited a region filled with precious resources[34] and numerous miraculous springs.[35] The land abundantly provides resources and wealth often of superior quality[36] for its inhabitants who also live free from many diseases and ailments (F45 §32). In essence, the lands at the edge of the world are often seen as utopic realms where people live justly while the land provides their sustenance and wealth in plenty (F45 §26).[37]

The *Indika*, however, was not a mere collection of marvels, as the fragments seemingly indicate. Ctesias devoted large portions of the work to the customs of the Indians with no indication of any fantastic elements involved (F45 §16, 30). Unfortunately, later authors citing the *Indika* were more interested in marvels and showed little concern for such mundane details. The loss of these parts of the *Indika* is irreparable, since Ctesias in all probability obtained at least some of his information directly from Indians themselves. He certainly had the opportunity to meet several Indian travellers at the Persian court as he himself acknowledges.[38] That Photius mentions Ctesias' discussion of their customs several times indicates that Ctesias devoted a substantial portion of his work to this topic and returned to it on multiple occasions.[39]

One digression on Indian customs may have been part of a larger discussion on Indian medicine, much of which was passed over by later excerpters. Photius tells us that Ctesias, while describing Indian habits, mentions their disdain for death (F45 §30). This is followed in the fragments by several sections in which medicinal topics frequently recur. First there is a spring from which a truth serum is derived (§31), followed by what was evidently a more mundane investigation into Indian medicine (§32), two types of poison (§33, 34), and a remedy for bowel irritation (§35).[40] This focus on medicine is perhaps not merely the result of personal interest. He certainly would have been constantly vigilant for new and more effective remedies for ailments, especially with the powerful clientele he served. Ctesias' statement that the Indians do not suffer from 'headaches, ophthalmia, toothaches, cold-sores, or putrefaction' (§32), surely is the result of the physician's inquiry into the subject, as such specific information could hardly have been volunteered by the visitors. This passage may help shed light on some of the common ailments suffered in fifth-century Persia, but one can only wonder what valuable information was omitted. Unfortunately, Photius and the other excerpters were more interested in the fantastic aspect of these medical explanations, choosing to pass over much of this testimony.

While later authors showed a predilection for the marvels of the *Indika,* many of which were rooted in fact but took on fantastic elements through oral tradition, Ctesias was strikingly accurate when he was able to view things firsthand.[41] His description of the elephant, although containing some misinformation,[42] is for the most part correct.[43] His account of the parrot is not only accurate, but given with enough detail that one may even speculate on the species.[44] However, to his Greek audience, these creatures belonged to the same world of fantasy as the martichora or the unicorn. For Ctesias, seeing such marvels certainly would have increased his gullibility regarding the other seemingly incredible stories he heard. After all, if India had brilliantly coloured birds which could speak a human language, certainly it was plausible that other such marvels which he was not able to view could exist.

Ctesias' sources

It is unlikely that Ctesias had access to any written literature from the Indian subcontinent. Nowhere in the fragments do we find a reference to written sources; rather, Ctesias' text suggests that all the information he received directly from the Indians was of an oral nature.

As some passages of his *Indika* clearly indicate,[45] Ctesias must have been acquainted with the oral traditions that later gave shape to literary creations such as the great epics *Mahābhārata* and *Rāmāyana*. The *Mahābhārata* is ascribed to the legendary sage Vyāsa who is also credited with the organization of the Vedas into four texts, while the *Rāmāyana* was composed by Vālmīki, perhaps a near contemporary of Ctesias. Both works began to circulate orally after the end of the Vedic Age in the sixth century BCE and underwent extensive development over a long period of time between the fifth century BCE and the fourth century CE.[46] Similarly, other Indian works such as the *Upanishads,* the secret teachings and philosophy of the sages of the late Vedic Age,[47] and the *Purānas* (religious Hindu texts),[48] have their beginnings in oral transmissions predating the earliest manuscripts by several centuries. Ctesias was thus historically positioned to encounter – and use in his work – some of the oral literature from India which was beginning to circulate in his time.

The sources used by Ctesias for his description of India seem to have varied greatly. According to Ctesias himself, his main source was autopsy and firsthand accounts from people he met at the Persian court (F45 §51). However, he clearly made some use of his Greek predecessors as well as artistic representations he had seen while in Persia. Each of these needs to be examined separately.

Ctesias invokes autopsy on several different occasions in the *Indika*. He claims to have seen several artifacts from India and even sampled a few products. He maintains that the cheese and wine of India are exceedingly sweet (F45 §48) and the sweet-smelling oil of the *karpion* has a fragrance that defies description (F45 §47). He claims to have seen the astragalos of the unicorn (F45 §45) and a young martichora (F45 §15). Ctesias says that the Persian king possessed dung pellets of the *dikairon* bird which were used as a drug for euthanasia (F45m) and as the royal physician may reasonably have had a chance to view them. He would have been able to bring some objects back to Greece including the swords he received from the king and the queen mother which were fashioned from Indian iron (F45 §9).

Ctesias also certainly received many of his accounts from travellers to the Persian court. He mentions on several occasions the Indians he encountered during his residency at the various capitals of the Persian Empire.[49] In Babylon, he obtained a viewing of an elephant in the care of an Indian mahout (F45bα) and his assertion that the parrot speaks Indian suggests that he saw one in the custody of an Indian handler (F45 §8). His accurate account on the practice of falconry (F45g) may have resulted from witnessing a demonstration by an Indian (or perhaps Bactrian) falconer. Elsewhere in an effort to refute Herodotus' arguments regarding the skin colour of the Indians, he claims to have encountered seven light-skinned Indians (F45 §19). There is no reason to doubt his assertions since we know from Achaemenid reliefs that there were Indian visitors to the Persian court usually bringing gifts.[50]

In addition to Indian travellers, Bactrian merchants visiting the Persian palaces who were readily involved in trade with the Indians, proved to be a major source for Ctesias' conception of India. Bactria formed a crossroads between India and the Middle East becoming an important trading centre in exotic goods along the Silk Road which passed from China and north India through Bactria and into the Iranian Plateau.[51] Bactrian contact with the Indus Valley as early as the Middle Bronze Age has been confirmed by the discovery of a Harappan settlement in Eastern Bactria at Shortughaï.[52] Since Bactria was within the realm of the Persian Empire and a tributary to the king, Bactrian visitors conveying East Asian wares to the Persian court were probably frequent.

The fantastic image of India held by the Persians (and Ctesias) was probably encouraged by these merchants who no doubt would relate (or perhaps at times even fabricate) the mythical background of their goods in order to increase their value.[53] For example, Ctesias says that the *pantarbe* gemstone (F45 §6) which possesses magnetic qualities and is used to retrieve other gems from the Indus, belonged to a Bactrian merchant. It seems evident that it was the merchant himself who showed Ctesias the stone and informed him of its magnificent properties. Since there is no known object in Indian literature or archaeology to serve as a basis for this stone, its fantastic properties may have originated with the Bactrians (perhaps even with the merchant himself). Similarly, his information of the silver mines of India (F45 §26) comes from Bactrians who, although attesting to the abundance of silver in India, naturally professed the superiority of their own mines.

At times Ctesias' Bactrian sources may also have been relating information based on their own mythology or interests. It is possible that some of Ctesias' reports of snakes and serpents (ex. F45 §33 and F45l; F45 §46 and F45r), although likely of Indian origin (see notes), came from Bactrians who certainly had a predilection for the creatures.[54] Ctesias credits the Bactrians as his source on the griffins which guard the gold in India (F45 §26 and F45h). Although his description of the griffin accords with the Greek conception of this beast in the fifth century, there is no reason to doubt that he is relating an authentic Bactrian tradition of the animal.[55] His vivid description with focus on specific colours and the reference (albeit a vague one) to an artisan has lead many to argue that he saw the griffin depicted on a piece of artwork. Although a likely hypothesis, the artwork in question need not have been Greek, as has often been supposed.[56]

Similarly, Ctesias' description of the Pygmies (F45 §21; F45f α-γ) seems on first glance to have been influenced by Greek artwork. He describes them as being exceedingly small with ugly, snub-nosed faces and thick penises which reach their ankles, and they grow their hair and beards to their feet, binding them at the waist in lieu of clothing. With the exception of their hair and beards which appear nowhere in Greek art, his description seems to conform to the Greek conception of dwarves who are often depicted on vases, lamps, and figurines[57] with large penises and snub-nosed faces. Although such depictions are rare before the Hellenistic period,[58] they do appear in Athens during the fifth century.[59] However, contextually they have little in common with the Pygmies of Ctesias. In Greek art, dwarves are often shown in a comical light, but at the same time were considered apotropaic[60] while their large penises were often seen as symbolic of their sexual virility.[61] None of these characteristics comports to the Pygmies of Ctesias of whom nothing comical or apotropaic was implied. Nor was there indication of their sexual prowess which Ctesias certainly would have mentioned had he intended such a distinction to be made.[62]

Near Eastern works of art certainly played a prominent role in shaping Ctesias' view of some of the creatures found in the *Indika*. Many of the peoples and animals he described are hybrids of men with animal features, animals with human features, or animals with features of other species, all of which are motifs of Near Eastern art. An Eastern artifact may have influenced his account of the martichora which he describes as the size of a lion with a human face and scorpion stingers on the tail (F45 §15) with the paws of a lion (F45dβ).[63] The concept of an animal with a human face was common to Near Eastern art, most notably in the sphinx.[64] Similarly, Ctesias' account of the Cynocephaloi conforms to the Near Eastern motif of humans with animal heads.[65] Other hybrids widely found in Near Eastern art resulted from the combination of multiple animals, a recurring theme in the *Indika* with creatures such as the griffin and martichora.[66]

Possibly the most telling evidence that Ctesias made extensive use of artistic representations for his information on India is his strict attention to colour. He tries to be as specific as possible when describing colours, often comparing them to colours more familiar to his Greek audience. Several times he employs the phrase 'red like cinnabar' when describing objects and animals he had evidently seen personally;[67] however he gives equal attention to other colours. When giving a detailed account of an object or animal he had the chance to encounter, Ctesias often focuses intently on its colours. He vividly describes the variegated plumes of the parrot (F45 §8) and the Indian cock (F45bβ) and claims to have seen an astragalos of the unicorn (F45 §45) adding that it is 'the colour of cinnabar'.[68]

In most cases this concentration on specific colours must be the result of viewing a piece of artwork for which he evidently had a certain affinity. He professes a fondness for Indian tapestries and garments which he claims are superior to those of the Persians (F45 §39), an opinion possibly shared by the Persians themselves (F45pγ). He maintains that the crimson (porphyry) dyes used by the Indians are equal to those of the Greeks but brighter (F45 §38). Based on the details he gives, he may have seen some of the animals of his India on these tapestries. For example, he describes the Indian serpent as having a 'body like beautiful crimson' (F45 §33) and a head that is 'not off-white, so to speak, but a white brighter than snow or milk' (F45l). Similarly, the *dikairon* bird is said to be the colour of realgar, which is an orange-red (F45m), a colour relatively rare in the Greek sources.

Influence of the work

The *Indika* had a profound influence on subsequent generations. As it was the first document written by a westerner on India, the work was integral in shaping the Greek conception of what was an unknown land thought to be on the edges of the earth. It was only after the campaigns of Alexander reached the Indus Valley that many of his accounts were proven to be purely myth. However, many aspects of the *Indika* continued to be taken as fact by later writers, including scientists such as Aristotle and Megasthenes, the ambassador of Seleucus Nicator to the court of Sandrocottus (Chandragupta Maurya). At times the veracity of Ctesias could be corroborated, such as with the parrot or the elephant, while in other instances his testimony was simply accepted. However, it was in genres beyond the scientific realm including the novel and paradoxography where the *Indika* had the greatest impact.

Until Alexander's campaign along the Indus in 326-325 BCE, Ctesias was the authority on India. As a pupil of Aristotle, Alexander himself was certainly familiar with Ctesias' writings. He had a certain fascination for India which stemmed not only from the scientific inquisitiveness instilled in him by his famed teacher, but undoubtedly from reading the fanciful tales of India found in Ctesias, Scylax, and Herodotus. As a Greek he certainly had a conventional idea of India before his arrival.[69] His fascination with India led him to bring a retinue of such scientists as Callisthenes and Onesicritus on his campaign to study this mysterious land. In fact, curiosity about the unknown edges of the world, coupled perhaps with an insatiable desire for conquest, are what drove Alexander to invade India, since by crossing the Indus he went beyond the limits of the Persian Empire, his original objective.[70]

Aristotle's familiarity with Ctesias is well attested in the fragments. Although he frequently viewed Ctesias with suspicion (F45dα; F45kα), he certainly accepted some of his testimony as trustworthy. He used Ctesias as his main source for his accurate description of the elephant.[71] Like Ctesias (F45bα), Aristotle says the elephant tears down walls and can uproot a palm (*HA* 610a19; *PA* 659a1), but only names Ctesias directly when refuting him on a specific point (F48a and F48b) or to express disbelief.[72] Although sceptical, he apparently found the fantastic martichora plausible enough to warrant a description (F45dα). Elsewhere he seems to accept Ctesias' testimony with a little more certainty. His accounts of the Indian ass, which include a discussion of the astragalos (*HA* 499b18) and the solid hoofs (*PA* 663a18), are surely based on Ctesias, although with some reservations expressed.[73] He certainly follows Ctesias for his account of the parrot (*HA* 597b27) although the variant name he gives for the bird suggests that he may have used an additional source.[74] It is clear that Aristotle had a relatively low opinion of Ctesias overall, but found some elements of his work plausible and reliable, especially since he had so little else to rely on for India.

Megasthenes, writing a century after Ctesias, frequently gave different accounts of marvels found in Ctesias because of his desire to refute him.[75] He would often choose to follow Greek traditions other than Ctesias,[76] but would readily accept some of Ctesias' testimony when none else existed while still attempting to improve upon it. For instance, he gives accounts of the lofty Indian reed (*FGrH* 715 F27b) similar to that of

Ctesias (F45 §14; F45c) but adds greater detail. Whereas Ctesias says that the reeds 'are as thick as two men's embrace and as high as the mast of a large tonnage merchant ship' and are used to make riverboats (*Persika* F1b §17.5), Megasthenes describes the same reeds but gives precise measurements saying they were up to thirty *orgyiae* tall (*c.* 180 feet) and up to 6 cubits in diameter. Similarly, he accepts the veracity of the unicorn[77] (*FGrH* 715 F27b) but seems to be relating a different tradition, perhaps one of Indian origin in which he refers to the creature as the *kartazon*.[78] He refers to the creature as a horse instead of an ass, having yellow or auburn hair, a pig's tail and black horn. However, there are certain details in his description which suggest that he was viewing this creature in light of what he had read in Ctesias. Since he was not a physician he ignores the specific medicinal and antidotal powers of the horn, claiming simply that it was invincible. In a similar fashion, both authors discuss the difficulties in hunting the beast. Whereas Ctesias states that the unicorn can only be captured when it is with its young, Megasthenes says that it is only the young who can be captured. Finally, Megasthenes states that the *kartazon* had non-jointed feet like the elephant. This particular statement seems to be a direct attack on Ctesias who claimed to have personally seen an astragalos of the unicorn and apparently went to great lengths in describing its beauty.

After the campaigns of Alexander Megasthenes became the authority on India and Ctesias' *Indika* was relegated to the world of folklore and the newly developing genre of paradoxography. Paradoxography, a modern term used to describe the writing of *Wonder-Books* or the collections of *mirabilia*,[79] became a fully developed genre in the third century BCE. While interest in the fantastic is as old as Greek literature itself,[80] and perhaps even older,[81] it is only with the advent of paradoxography that entire works were devoted to the subject. Previously, marvels were either relegated to the mythological world of the remote past (e.g. Homer's *Odyssey*) or given a place only as digressions in more 'serious' works of history (e.g. Herodotus). The most striking example of the latter is Theopompus who, writing almost a half-century after Ctesias, devoted all of Book 8 (and perhaps some of Book 9) of his *Philippica* to a collection of marvels.[82]

Although the *Indika* does not fall into the category of paradoxography, it was the earliest work for which we have any significant knowledge to give such a prominent place to marvels within the contemporary world and would lay the foundations for the full development of the genre.[83] Like the paradoxographers, Ctesias was describing wonders belonging to the real contemporary world. His focus on a particular region was adopted by several later paradoxographers such as Nymphodoros (Sicily) and Philon (Scythia). His attention to unusual plants, animals and bodies of water as well as peoples with extraordinary physiology and customs became the basic content of paradoxographical works[84] while his emphasis on credibility became a hallmark of the genre.[85] Callimachus, the Alexandrian librarian who has often been credited as originator of the field,[86] cited his literary predecessors excessively since he was unable to witness his marvels firsthand, a practice followed by many of his successors.[87]

Chief among his sources on India, despite the availability of more reliable authors, was Ctesias.[88]

During the Roman period India was still the land of fable and folklore that it was during the time of Ctesias.[89] The *Indika* was still used as a source on India by authors of natural history and zoology (Pliny, Aelian),[90] although at times with suspicion. Ctesias, as a man of science, had a certain predilection for natural history, shown by the fact that the flora and fauna of the region play a central role in his treatise.[91] The *Indika* thus contained many elements which would have been of interest to a natural historian. By this time his reputation as a historian was tarnished beyond repair[92] and it seems that any credibility he still enjoyed was in the world of natural history. For example, Aelian follows his account on several Indian animals and peoples such as the elephant (F45bα) and the Cynocephaloi (F45pγ) without any hint of suspicion. Similarly, Pliny often accepts his testimony as fact with no doubt expressed such as with Sciapodes (F51a) and the *pitthachora* tree (F45oα). Both authors readily accept the veracity of the martichora (F45dβ, F45d δ) while Pausanias, another author of the same period whose scope resides outside of the field of natural history, doubts the credibility of the same passage (F45dγ).

During this same period, the works of Ctesias had an even bigger impact on the ancient novel. The *Persika* was the more influential work as the dramatic style employed by Ctesias had a profound effect on the development of fictional writing beginning in the Hellenistic period.[93] While the *Indika* was undoubtedly composed in the same clear and simple style for which Ctesias has been admired,[94] as an ethnographic treatise with no mention of any specific characters it lacks the dramatic element so prominent in the *Persika*. However, the *Indika* would be used by writers of fiction to set the background for many of their tales. Early recensions of the *Alexander Romance* made extensive use of the *Indika* to form the basis of Alexander's adventures in India.[95] Similarly, Philostratus reproduced many of the wonders found in the *Indika* when describing Apollonius' travels in India. He mentions the martichora (3.45), the *pantarbe* stone (3.46), the Indus worm (3.1), and the unicorn (3.2), to name a few. Philostratus often repeats what Ctesias says nearly verbatim indicating that he was taking these marvels directly from the pages of the *Indika*. Lucian mentions only Ctesias and Iamboulus as sources in the introduction to his *Verae Historiae* (T11h). He says that Ctesias wrote about things in India that he neither saw firsthand nor heard about from a reliable source lampooning the final statement of the *Indika* (F45 §51).

By late antiquity, marvels from Ctesias' India began to appear in collections such as the *Physiologus* and the *Etymologiae* of Isidore of Seville. Fantastic animals such as the martichora[96] and the unicorn are described and would become mainstays throughout medieval literature. Monstrous creatures and fabulous races of men such as the Cynocephaloi became fixtures in medieval bestiaries; however they usually reached the authors of the Middle Ages through intermediaries such as Pliny, Solinus and Isidore.[97] Many of these fabulous races appear in the fantastic travel books of John Mandeville and Marco Polo. Ctesias' monsters, including the Sciapodes, unicorns, and long-eared people, were regularly placed in India on Medieval maps of the world such as the thirteenth century Hereford map.[98] Similarly, Ctesianic creatures often appeared in the visual arts including the martichora, the long-eared people, the Cynocephaloi, and those with eyes on their shoulders, just to name a few.[99] The more popular beasts, such as the unicorn, the martichora, and the eagle-headed griffin have survived into the twentieth century in Jose Luis Borges' *El Libro de los Seres Imaginarios*.

Minor works

In addition to the *Indika* and the *Persika*, Ctesias authored several lesser known treatises which are poorly preserved, even in fragmentary form. Little can be discerned as to their content or quality (or for that matter if they even existed). Of the scant remains the two best preserved works are *On the Tributes of Asia* and the *Periodos* (also called the *Periegesis* and the *Periplous*). Very little is known of the former work (F53, F54), however based on the title it seems to have been a work devoted to the various tributaries of the Persian Empire. The loss of this work is irreparable since Ctesias was in a unique position to list the various nations within the empire and perhaps shed some light on what each contributed to the king. The meagre remains of the work indicate that there may have been some focus on the alimentary contributions each nation made to the king's elaborate dinner.[100] This work, however, must have covered a wider range of topics with ethnographical digressions on each nation.

A little more light can be shed on the *Periodos* since it is in a slightly better state of preservation (F55-F60). Based on the title, it seems to have been a geographical treatise covering all of Asia (F60) containing at least three books. Ctesias touched upon Egypt in Book I (F55) and Italy in Book III (F59) though this latter mention may have been a passing reference as a digression on Umbria would not be suitable to a work on Asia. Although the overall content cannot be weighed, it is certain that Ctesias dealt at length with the Black Sea region.[101] He discussed tribes from the area in Book I (F56) and Book II (F57-F58). He may then have begun his *Periodos* in Egypt and then worked his way up the coast through the Levant to the Black Sea. He reached the Black Sea from the south (F56) then seems to have circumnavigated the sea[102] before heading east.

Ctesias may also have written one or more medical treatises (F67-F68)[103] of which little survives. Based on the minimal remnants of the works, only a little can be discerned as to their nature and content. The medical writings seem to be standard medical compositions with no references to Ctesias' stay at the Persian court. They may thus have been composed before he left Greece, though this is pure speculation. In one work he criticizes Hippocrates' methods of setting a dislocated hip, which is not surprising since he was a member of the Cnidian school of medicine which rivalled that of Hippocrates' Cos.[104] In the other work, Ctesias discusses the use of hellebore, a plant commonly used in Greek medicine by the end of the fifth century.[105] He claims that while it was dangerous in his father's time, it was safe in his day thus expressing the medical advances achieved in the fifth century.

The essays *On Mountains* (F73) and *On Rivers* (F74) have been deemed spurious by Jacoby, despite the fact that they are both mentioned by title. Although they are unattested elsewhere, which certainly renders their existence as individual works suspect, the content of their fragments show that they come from genuine works of Ctesias. Both compositions discuss medicinal cures found in nature. The former describes a stone used to treat leprosy and the latter a plant which when boiled down can cure madness.[106] Since works in the ancient world were not always clearly titled, it is possible that Plutarch, the author responsible for both fragments, simply referred to a sub-section of a larger work by their more specific headings.[107] The titles used by Plutarch, even if arbitrarily, seemingly rule out the hypothesis that these fragments come from a medical treatise. If not independent, then the works would best fit in with the *Periodos* since they are both of a geographical nature. In both cases Ctesias is not only focusing on the medicinal benefits of the objects in question but their origins as well. In any case, if these were isolated treatises, they, like the *Periodos* and *On the Tributes of Asia*, seem to have been of a more serious nature and consequently never achieved the popularity of the *Persika* and the *Indika*.

Notes

1. Scylax of Caryanda, the Greek navigator who sailed the Indus during the reign of Darius I, apparently wrote a treatise on his expedition, of which only a few passing references have survived. Like Ctesias, Scylax may have described India as a land of marvels which had their origins with Indian sources, such as the Otoliknoi (F51b). However, Herodotus (4.44),

who gives the earliest account of Scylax, makes no mention of his treatise or any indication that such a work existed.

2. The *editio princeps* of the *Bibliotheca* of Photius edited by David Hoeschel did not appear until 1601. The first real critical edition of the *Bibliotheca* was produced by August Immanuel Bekker in 1824-1825.

3. Janick Auberger (1991) published a French translation with a basic commentary of all the fragments based on Jacoby's edition.

4. Jacoby acknowledges that Nicolaus was using Ctesias as his source but nevertheless published the fragments of his work separately.

5. Cf. Jacoby 1922 col. 2036.

6. See for example the studies of Brown (1978) and Eck (1990).

7. The statement of Tzetzes (T1b) that Ctesias was from the Cyprian colony of the same name is clearly false. Ctesias, a noted physician from a family with a long history in medicine was a member of the Cnidian school of medicine which was based in the Carian city of Asia Minor. On Cnidus as a centre for the study of medicine see Kollesch 1989.

8. By Ctesias' time the Persian kings had long been employing Greek physicians at the court. The first Greek to hold such a position was Democedes (cf. Hdt. 3.129-33) who served under Darius I. He was followed by Apollonides of Cos (F14 §34, 44) who was ultimately buried alive after allegedly defiling the daughter of Artaxerxes I.

9. Müller (1844 p. 2) even proposed to emend the text of Diodorus to read seven years rather than seventeen years for the duration of Ctesias' stay in Persia (cf. Bigwood 1978 pp. 19-20 and n. 3). However, the manuscripts are unanimous on this point and there is no reason to suspect corruption (cf. Stronk 2007 pp. 37-8 and n. 50). In fact, the figure of seventeen years is corroborated by Tzetzes (T1b). Although Tzetzes may have been using Diodorus for this information, to follow Mueller's emendation one would have to adhere to the unlikely assumption that Tzetzes was reading a manuscript with the same textual error which has come down to us. Jacoby (1922 col. 2033) accepts the text as is but contends that Ctesias exaggerates the length of his stay at the court in order to profess superiority over his predecessors, namely Apollonides of Cos.

10. Cf. Brown (1978 pp. 8-10) who suggests that Ctesias was taken prisoner by Tissaphernes while serving as a volunteer in the army of Pissouthnes, the satrap of Lydia, when the latter revolted from Persian authority (*c.* 413 BCE). His knowledge of medicine probably saved his life when it caught the attention of the new satrap. According to Brown, he would have come into the service of the king in 404 BCE when

Tissaphernes met Artaxerxes in Babylon thus accounting for his focus on the reign of Artaxerxes (see also Eck 1990 pp. 431-2 for a similar theory).

11. It is doubtful that the Persian king would allow a complete stranger and newcomer to the court to be his personal physician. Rather, it is more plausible that Ctesias would have to earn the trust of the king and prove his abilities by working his way up the court hierarchy before being placed in charge of the king's health.

12. cf. T7aα.

13. F15 §50-1, 56; cf. Brosius 1996 p. 110.

14. Some scholars contend that Diodorus and Tztetzes both believed that Ctesias was in the service of Cyrus and captured by Artaxerxes at Cunaxa (cf. Bähr 1824 pp. 13-15; König p. 1 n. 17; Jacoby 1922 col. 2033-5 argues that both authors were mistaken in their belief). This contention is impossible since Plutarch (T6aα; T6b; T7b) and Xenophon (T6aβ) both clearly show that Ctesias was serving on the side of Artaxerxes when the battle commenced. For one, Plutarch's statement that Ctesias was honoured after the battle would hardly have been plausible for a captive from the enemy's side, even if he did treat the king's wound. Moreover, as a member of Cyrus' army, Xenophon would surely have indicated if Ctesias were among their number. The strong showing of the Greek forces at Cunaxa offers no real chance for a Greek to be taken captive during the battle.

15. Cf. Bigwood 1995 p. 140.

16. Cf. Brown 1978 p. 13.

17. He also no doubt would have still been incensed over the large role played by Spartan mercenaries in the army of Cyrus. While Darius had formed an alliance with Sparta against Athens towards the end of the Peloponnesian War, Artaxerxes had ample reasons, aside from personal enmity, for rejecting this alliance now that the political climate in Greece had changed so drastically.

18. Brown (1978 p. 18 n. 83) suggests that the note was conciliatory in nature, perhaps a renewal of their alliance, but admits that Artaxerxes had motives to be surreptitious.

19. This would include the *Persika*, the *Indika*, the *Periplous*, and *On the Tributes in Asia*. It is uncertain when he composed any of his medical treatises (if in fact he composed any – cf. F67, F68 and notes). He may also have continued to practise medicine since not many of his rivals could boast having tended to the Great King of Persia (cf. Brown 1978 p. 19).

20. Ctesias (F27 §71) makes reference to the palms which appeared

over the tomb of Clearchos eight years after his death. Since Clearchos died in 401 BCE, the palms would have materialized in the year 393/392 BCE. König (1972 p. 26 n. 13) takes this to mean that Ctesias did not leave Persia until after this time and consequently places his arrival at the royal court in 409 BCE. He believes then that Ctesias returned to Persia after serving on the embassy to Evagoras and Sparta, but for reasons left unexplained still only covered events up to 398/397 in his work (nor does he offer up a scenario in which Ctesias may have escaped in 393/392). Such a line of argument has rightly been rejected by scholars. It is clear that Ctesias merely heard about the palms from a secondhand source, possibly after the Battle of Cnidus in 394. This passage does, however, indicate that the *Persika* was not completed before 393 BCE (cf. Brown 1978 p. 6).

21. Cf. Eck 1990 p. 413.

22. Artaxerxes built a new palace at Susa (*A²Sd*) and rebuilt the *apadana* (audience hall) of Darius I which was destroyed by fire during the reign of Artaxerxes I (*A²Sa*). On the new palace at Susa see the study of Boucharlat and Labrousse (1979); on the inscriptions see Vallat (1979) and Kent (1953 pp. 154-5).

23. According to an inscription (*A²Hb*), Artaxerxes constructed an *apadana* at Ecbatana. However, this project was more likely a restoration of the apadana first built by Darius I. The fact that Persepolis and probably Susa had only one apadana make it all but certain that only one ever existed in Ecbatana; cf. Stronach (1987); for text and translation of the inscription see Kent (1953 p. 155).

24. Unlike his predecessors, he was not buried at *Naqši-Rustam* but nearby on what became known as the royal hill (cf. Diod. 17.71.7; on his tomb see the study of Schmidt 1970 pp. 99-102).

25. Cf. F45bα where he claims that he witnessed an elephant uproot a date-palm in Babylon.

26. Cf. Eck 1991 p. 413; however, it has recently been shown that he was responsible for the construction of a new palace in Babylon as well; cf. Vallat 1989.

27. Cf. Bigwood 1978b pp. 32-3.

28. Cf. Olmstead 1948 p. 375.

29. F28; cf. Eck 1990 pp. 413-14.

30. Cf. Jacoby 1922.

31. For instance, his account of the *Henotiktontes* and the *Enotokoitai* certainly originated in the subcontinent as both are well attested in Indian

literature; cf. F45 §50 and notes. To the Indians of the subcontinent, the northwest region and Indus Valley was also a land of marvels and fantasy, just as it was for the Greeks and Persians.

32. The Indians can live as long as 200 years (F45 §32) as can the Cynocephaloi (F45 §43).

33. The Indians as a whole are described as just on no less than three occasions (F45 §16, 20, 30 where he evidently spoke at length on their righteousness) and several times specific tribes are referred to as just. The just nature of the Pygmies (F45 § 23) and the Cynocephaloi (F45 §37, 43; F45pβ-γ) is heavily emphasized.

34. Cf. F45 §6, 9, 11, etc.

35. Ctesias had a predilection for springs mentioning no fewer than ten of them.

36. Cf. F45 §25 on Indian oil, §47 on the perfume from the *karpion*, §48 on their wine and cheese.

37. Cf. Lenfant (1995 pp. 325-7); On the topoi of the fringes of the earth see Karttunen (2002 esp. pp. 463-5).

38. Cf. F45 §18; He also saw an elephant accompanied by an Indian mahout give a demonstration of its strength (F45bα).

39. Cf. F45 §23 where he discusses the customs of the Pygmies as being the same as the rest of the Indians. He may have elaborated or given a more detailed account of the mores shared by the two.

40. Undeniably Ctesias' interest in medicine is evident throughout the *Indika*. For instance, he speaks of the antidotal powers of the unicorn horn, which he also maintains cures epilepsy (F45 §45). He mentions a fountain with fantastic properties, finishing the description by saying it cures the so-called white disease (F45sα; see note). However, the recurring appearance of medicine in these sequential passages introduced by the discussion on the Indians' contempt for death points to the possibility that he devoted an entire section of his work to Indian medicine, something to be expected of a physician; cf. F45l where Aelian seems to acknowledge that Ctesias' explanation of the crimson snake comes amid a discourse on medicine.

41. See for example his account on falconry (Cf. F45 §24; F45g and notes).

42. Cf. F48a-b and notes.

43. Cf. F45 §7; F45bα and notes.

44. Cf. F45 §8 and notes. Unfortunately, problems with the text prevent any identification with certainty; cf. Bigwood (1993b), Romm (1992).

45. e.g. F45 §7, §44, §50 (see notes), etc.

46. Cf. Brockington (2003 pp. 116-17); see also Goldman (2005 pp. 16-17) who dates the origins of the *Rāmāyana* to around the middle of the fourth century BCE.

47. Although the textual transmission of the *Upanishads* has suffered due to their secretive nature, it is clear that they originated in the Vedic period and, like the epics, developed over the succeeding centuries. They are traditionally viewed as the 'end of the Veda' – *Vedānta* (see Witzel 2003 pp. 83-7).

48. According to the Matsya *Purāna* (53.3-4), the *Purānas,* like the *Mahābhārata,* were first compiled by Vālmīki. Like the epics, they originated as oral performances by the bards at the courts of the *kshatriya* nobility (see Matchett 2003 pp. 130-2).

49. The Persian monarch had several royal palaces placed strategically throughout the empire in cities such as Susa, Pasargadae, Babylon, Persepolis and Ecbatana. The king would move about the empire taking up residency at the various palaces throughout the year, although some kings would favour certain capitals to the neglect of others (see the study of Briant 1988 on the movements of the Great King throughout the empire). As royal physician, Ctesias would certainly accompany Artaxerxes wherever he went and so had the opportunity to visit more than one Persian capital. See above pp. 17-18.

50. See for example the procession reliefs at Persepolis; cf. Schmidt (1970 pp. 151-2); Root (1979 pp. 227-84).

51. Zhang Qian, the Chinese emissary during the Han Dynasty (first century BCE) who was sent along the Silk Road, famously recorded his visit to Bactria (Daxia); the account survives in the *Shiji* of Sima Qian. However, the discovery of Chinese silk dating from the Middle Bronze Age indicates that Bactria was an important trading post along the Silk Road early on (cf. Whitfield and Sims-Williams 2004 p. 46)

52. By 2000 BCE the settlement had become Bactrian in culture. See the studies of Gardin (1997 pp. 68, 76-7) and Francfort (1978-1979 pp. 91-4; 1983 pp. 518-19).

53. See for example the goods associated with the Cynocephaloi, which Ctesias seems to have viewed firsthand (F45 §40-1).

54. See for example the study of Sarianidi 1998 pp. 34-7; similarly other animals found in the *Indika* of Indian origin such as monkeys appear in early Bactrian art (ibid. 42).

55. See note on F45 §26 for a full discussion of the evidence.

56. e.g. Lenfant (2004 p. 324 n. 912).

57. See for example Robertson (1979); for depictions on lamps see Grandjouan (1961).

58. Cf. Shapiro (1984 p. 391).

59. See for example the fragment of a red-figure cup showing two dwarves dancing in Hornbostel and Kropatschek (1980 pp. 142-3). However, his equation of them with Pygmies is certainly in error since, with the exception of their snub-noses, they bear no resemblance to either the Homeric or Ctesianic Pygmies. Unlike the Pygmies of Ctesias, these dwarves have short hair and beards and, although their penises are slightly larger than normal, they in no way reach their ankles.

60. Cf. Binsfeld (1956 pp. 43-4).

61. Cf. Robertson (1979 p. 130) corrected by Shapiro (1984).

62. For example see his discussion of the sexual habits of the Cynocephaloi (F45 §43).

63. Jacoby (1922 col. 2038) proposes that Ctesias may have seen an Indian artifact brought to Persia through the trade network. However, the hybrid motif so common in Persian art coupled with the clearly Persian name of the beast (see note on F45 §15) suggests a Persian artifact as a more plausible source (cf. Müller 1844 p. 92b following Bähr 1824).

64. See for example the *lamassu* (guardian figure) found in Throne Room VII of the Palace of Sargon at Khorsabad; cf. Loud (1936 p. 38 fig. 45); Moortgat (1984 p. 125-6); see the similar figures at the entrance to 'Gate of All Nations' in Persepolis.

65. See for example the alabaster relief of the eagle-headed genius depictions from the Northwest Palace of Assurnasirpal II in Nimrud (Moortgat 1984 pp. 101-2, pl. 55); cf. the bird-man figures depicted on Bactrian seals and amulets (Sarianidi 1998 pp. 172-3 and fig. 916, etc.; see also in the same volume fig. 912 for the man with the head of a horned animal).

66. Bactrian seals and amulets were discovered depicting a winged lion with a snake for a tail (Sarianidi 1998 p. 294 fig. 1628). Another amulet (fig. 1624) shows a lion with what appears to be a scorpion's tail which bears a striking similarity to Ctesias' description of the martichora.

67. F45 §15 in reference to the martichora; §45 when describing the astragalos of the unicorn; see also F45 §8 for his description of the parrot. Although the text is corrupt, it can safely be assumed that he used the phrase 'red like cinnabar'; cf. Bigwood (1993b p. 324).

68. See Lenfant 1995 pp. 325-6.

69. Cf. Parker 2008 p. 33.

70. See the study of Stoneman 2008 pp. 67-72.

71. F45 §7, F45bα and notes; cf. Bigwood 1993a pp. 539-44; Scullard 1974 p. 37-52. Romm (1989 pp. 572-5) dismisses written evidence as a source and argues that Aristotle based his information on autopsy of an African elephant; however this line of argument has been adequately refuted by Bigwood (op. cit.).

72. Cf. Bigwood 1993a pp. 540-1.

73. In *PA* he expresses his caution with phrases such as 'the so-called Indian ass' (line 23 echoing the sentiment of line 19), however in *HA* such caution is absent; see also Pliny *NH* 8.31 which likewise is based on Ctesias; cf. Bigwood 1993a p. 541.

74. F45 §8 and note; cf. Bigwood 1993a p. 541 and Bigwood 1993b p. 322.

75. See for example *FGrH* 715 F11a §6; he differs from Ctesias in his account of Semiramis' invasion of India by having the Assyrian queen die before the campaign begins whereas Ctesias (F1b §16-19) describes her invasion as a failure followed by her return to Bactria (cf. Brown 1955 pp. 23-6). Her long march through the Gedrosian Desert related by Nearchos (*FGrH* 133 F3a and F3b) reflects a local tradition not found in any earlier Greek author. On the possible influence of Ctesias' account on Alexander see Henry 1947 p. 8.

76. Megasthenes (*FGrH* 715 F23a and F23b) opts to follow Herodotus' account of the gold-digging ants rather than Ctesias' gold-guarding griffins (F45 §26; see Brown 1955 pp. 29-30; however his experiences in India may have led him to adopt this account. Nearchos [*FGrH* 133 F8a and F8b] claims that the local inhabitants brought the Macedonians skins from the gold-digging ants as gifts). Although he accepts the veracity of the Pygmies (*FGrH* 715 F27a and F27b) whom he calls the Trispithamoi ('Three spans tall'), he reverts to the Homeric account of the Pygmies and Cranes which was omitted by Ctesias (cf. note on F45 §21). He may have given an account of the Cynocephaloi (Plin. *NH* 7.23 = F45pα) however the source of Pliny's narrative is ambiguous at this point. He mentions Megasthenes immediately prior to his description of the Cynocephaloi and Ctesias immediately after. In any case, the passage makes it clear that if Megasthenes did give an account of the Cynocephaloi he followed Ctesias closely (cf. Lenfant 2004 p. 326 n. 935).

77. On the influence of Ctesias' unicorn for later Greek and Latin writers see Bienveniste 1929 pp. 372-3.

78. Ael. *HA* 16.20 (Frag. XV.B in the translation of McCrindle; this passage is curiously omitted in the text of Jacoby). On the possible Sanskrit root of the word *kartazon*, see Charpentier (1911-1912 pp. 402-3); cf. Bienveniste (1929 pp. 374-6) on the possible pre Indo-European root of the term, however his proposal to emend the word to *kargazon* has found few adherents. He is right to postulate that Megasthenes is giving a description of an Indian rhinoceros in place of Ctesias' Iranian unicorn. For an updated bibliography on the topic see Panaino 2001 pp. 161-2 nn. 67-76.

79. The term was first used by Johannes Tzetzes (*Chil.* 2.35.151); cf. Ziegler 1949 col. 1137-8.

80. Cf. Giannini 1963; Schepens and Delcroix 1996 p. 380.

81. Cf. Espelosín 1994 p. 146.

82. *FGrH* 115 F64-77; on the 'Marvels' place within the *Philippica* see Shrimpton 1991 pp. 15-20. Theopompus, although showing a predilection for prophets and portents, employed many of the motifs common to *mirabilia* at the edges of the world, such as extreme longevity and an abundance of gold (F57).

83. The *Arimaspea* of Aristeas of Proconnesus may have been the first work of this nature (cf. Giannini 1963 pp. 252-3), however too little is known of this work to ascertain its content or nature. Aristeas himself is a figure rooted in folklore (Hdt. 4.13-15; Strab. 13.1.16; 14.1.18) further obscuring any knowledge of the man or his work.

84. F45 §51; cf. Espelosín 1994 Tzetz. *Chil.* 2.35.151 gives a list of *topoi* used by paradoxographers; see the study of Schepens-Delcroix 1996 pp. 380-2.

85. See Schepens-Delcroix 1996 pp. 382-9.

86. Cf. Zeigler 1949 col. 1140-1; Giannini 1963 pp. 248-9 and 1964.

87. Cf. Schepens-Delcroix 1996 pp. 383-6.

88. Cf. Fraser 1972 I p. 763; on the use of Ctesias by other paradoxographers see Jacoby 1922 col. 2073.

89. See especially the study of Parker 2008.

90. Cf. Jacoby 1922 col. 2037.

91. Cf. Parker 2008 p. 29.

92. See for instance Plut. *Art.* 1.4 = *FGrH* 688 F15a.

93. See *FGrH* 688 T12-14; cf. Holzberg 2003 629-32.

94. Cf. *FGrH 688* T12.

95. Cf. Stoneman 1994.

96. See the recent study of Causi (2003) for a full discussion of the martichora from Ctesias to the modern age.

97. Cf. Wittkower 1942 pp. 166-71.

98. As with the bestiaries, the marvels of the Hereford map likely reached its author through intermediaries, especially Solinus; cf. Wittkower 1942 pp. 174-6. The map along with texts and translations of the legends has been published by S.D. Westrem (2001).

99. e.g. the illustrations from the *Heydenwelt* of Herold (1554); the early fifteenth-century manuscript of Marco Polo's *Le Livre des Merveilles* (Ms. Fr. 2810 in Bibliothèque Nationale de France); see also the plates in Wittkower 1942.

100. Cf. Lenfant 2004 pp. clviii-clix, who rightly asserts that this work was probably more serious in nature than the tales of intrigue and romance which dominate the *Persika*. The same could be said for the *Periodos*.

101. Cf. F56-58 and notes.

102. Assuming that F57 is from the *Periodos* (it is never mentioned specifically) and that its content preceded that of F58, Ctesias would have circumnavigated the sea in a counterclockwise motion since he mentions Colchis before Tiriza which is located in modern Bulgaria; see notes on F57-F58. However, his direction could just as easily have been the reverse.

103. Bähr (1824 p. 20) posited the theory that Ctesias composed a medical treatise and this has generally been accepted (see for instance the text of Jacoby). However, Lenfant has recently cast doubt on this view suggesting instead that Ctesias' criticism of Hippocrates may have come from either the *Persika* or the *Indika*.

104. On his criticisms and the rivalry between the two schools see note on F67.

105. On hellebore see note on F68.

106. See notes on F73 and F74 for full discussions.

107. Much in the same way that the first six books of the *Persika* are known alternatively as the *Assyriaka*.

The *Indika*

F45. Phot. *Bibl.* 72 p. 45a21-50a4 (T10)

[Ctesias] says about the Indus River that it is forty stades wide
at its narrowest point and two hundred at its widest. (2) He
claims that the population of the Indians is nearly greater than
the rest of the world combined. (3) There is a worm which
inhabits the river and is the only animal to live in it, and (4)
no men live beyond India. (5) It does not rain but India is
irrigated by the river. (6) Ctesias describes a gemstone called
pantarba, which when it was thrown into the river, was
retrieved clinging together 477 gems and precious stones that
belonged to a Bactrian dealer.

(7) Ctesias describes the wall-destroying elephants, the
small monkeys with tails four cubits in length, (8) and roosters
of enormous size. There is a bird called the *bittakos* which has
a human voice, is capable of speech, and grows to the size of
a falcon. It has a crimson face and a black beard and is dark
blue as far as the neck ... like cinnabar. It can converse like a
human in Indian but if taught Greek, it can also speak Greek.

(9) There is a spring which throughout the year fills with
liquid gold and from it one hundred clay jugs are drawn
annually. The jugs must be made of clay since the gold
solidifies when drawn off and the vessel must be broken in
order to remove it. The spring is square with a perimeter of

sixteen cubits and a depth of one *orgyia*. Each jug retrieves one talent of gold. There is iron at the bottom of the spring from which Ctesias says two swords were fashioned and given to him; one was from the king the other from the king's mother Parysatis. He maintains that the sword if stuck into the ground can ward off clouds, hail and hurricanes, an act he claims to have personally witnessed the king perform on two occasions. (10) The dogs in India are huge and they fight with lions. (11) There are large mountains where the sardonyx, the onyx, and other precious stones are quarried. (12) It is very hot there and the sun appears ten times larger than in any other land. Many people die of suffocation in these places. (13) Ctesias says that there is a sea there which is no smaller than the Greek Sea. Its surface up to four dactyls deep is so hot that no fish can approach the heat and survive so they all live below this level.

(14) The Indus River flows through the plains and mountains and the so-called Indian reed also grows there. These reeds are as thick as two men's embrace and as high as the mast of a large tonnage merchant ship. Some are even larger than this and some are smaller, such as is to be expected on a large mountain. The reeds can either be male or female. The male lacks a pith but is very strong whereas the female has a pith.

(15) There lives in India a beast called the martichora which has a human face, is the size of a lion, and is red like cinnabar. It has three rows of teeth, human ears, and light blue eyes like a man's. It has a tail like a land scorpion on which there is a stinger more than a cubit long. It also has stingers on either

side of the tail as well as on the end like a scorpion. If approached, it stabs with a stinger inflicting a fatal wound. If its opponent fights from a distance, then it points its tail at him and fires stingers as if from a bow, but when assailed from behind, it stretches its tail straight out. It can fire stingers as far as a *pletheron* and the stingers are completely fatal to everything except elephants. Each stinger is one foot long and as wide as the thinnest reed. The word 'martichora' means man-eater in Greek because it mostly captures and devours humans, but eats other animals as well. It fights with both its talons and stingers, which Ctesias claims grow back after being fired. Many of these creatures live in India where the natives kill them by firing arrows while riding elephants.

(16) Ctesias claims that the Indians are very just people; he also describes their customs and manners. (17) There is a holy place in the uninhabitable region where they honor Helios and Selene. This sanctuary is fifteen days journey from Mt. Sardo. For thirty-five days each year the sun cools in that region so that they can honour him with a festival and return home without being burned.

(18) There are no thunder, lightning, or heavy rainstorms in India, but heavy wind and hurricanes frequently wipe out whatever is in their path. The rising sun until midday stays cool, but for the rest of the day it causes severe heat for most of India. (19) Indians are not dark-skinned from the sun but by nature, for some of them, both men and women, are very light-skinned, even if they are a minority. Ctesias claims to have personally seen two such women and five such men of Indian stock. (20) In his desire to prove that the sun is cool in

India for thirty-five days, he says that the fire flowing from Aetna does not destroy the middle of the region because the men are just, although it destroys everything else. In Zacynthus, there is a spring filled with fish from which pitch is drawn. In Naxos, there is a spring from which sometimes flows a very sweet wine. Near Phaselis in Lycia, there is an unquenchable fire which burns night and day atop some rocks and it cannot be extinguished by water, which makes the flames burn brighter, but by rubbish.

(21) In the middle of India live black men called Pygmies who speak the same language as the rest of the Indians. They are very small; the tallest is two cubits while most are one and a half cubits in height. They have very long hair that reaches their knees and even lower and their beards are the longest of any man. Since they grow such a long beard, they wear no clothes at all but comb the hair from their head down their back well below their knees and pull their beards down the front to their feet and then gird the hair around their entire body using it in place of clothing. Their penises are so large that they reach their ankles and are thick too, while they themselves are snub-nosed and ugly. Their sheep are like lambs, their asses and oxen are nearly the size of rams, and their horses, mules, and all other livestock are no larger than rams. (23) Three thousand of those Pygmies accompany the king of the Indians, for they are excellent bowmen. They are very just and follow the same laws as the Indians. (24) They hunt hare and fox not with dogs, but with ravens, kites, crows, and eagles.

(25) There is a lake in their region with a perimeter of 800

stades on the surface of which oil settles when the wind is calm. They sail in skiffs through the middle of the lake and skim the oil from the surface with small cups and use it; they also use sesame oil. The lake also contains fish. They use oils from walnuts as well, but the oil from the lake is better.

(26) There is an abundance of silver in their region and the silver mines are not deep, but they say the mines in Bactria are deeper. There is gold in India but it is not found washed in the rivers as happens in the Pactolus River, rather it is found in the numerous large mountains where the griffins live. These are four-footed birds the size of a wolf with legs and claws like a lion. The feathers on the breast are red while those covering the rest of the body are black. Because of these creatures, it is hard to obtain the gold from the mountains, although it exists in large quantities.

(27) The sheep and goats of the Indians are larger than asses and they rear four to six offspring at most. They have large tails which they remove from those ripe for motherhood in order to assist in breeding. There is no swine either domesticated or wild in India. (28) The palms in India and their dates are three times the size of those in Babylon. (29) According to Ctesias, there is a river of honey which flows from a rock. (30) He speaks at length about the just nature of the Indians, the high regard they have for their king, and their disdain for death.

(31) There is a spring and when someone draws water from it, it solidifies like cheese. If you give someone three obols of this curdle to drink in water, he would tell you everything he has ever done, for it deprives him of his senses and sanity for

the entire day. The king uses this when he wants to discover the truth in allegations. If the accused confesses, he is ordered to starve himself to death, but if nothing is proved by this, he is acquitted.

(32) The Indians do not suffer from headaches, ophthalmia, toothaches, cold sores, or putrefaction. They live for 120, 130, and 150 years and some live to be as old as 200 years old.

(33) There lives in these parts a serpent which is a span in length and has a body like beautiful crimson and a bright white head. It has no teeth and is hunted in the burning mountains where the sardonyx is quarried. It does not bite but wherever it vomits, the entire area rots. It produces two fluids when hung by its tail: one is an amber-coloured substance and the other is black. The amber-coloured drug is extracted while the snake is still alive and the black drug after it is dead. When a sesame-seed size droplet of the poison extracted from the living snake is administered, the person who drank it immediately perishes with his brains flowing out through his nose. When the other poison is administered, it brings on consumption causing death in close to a year.

(34) There is a bird called the *dikairon* which in Greek means 'just'. It is the size of a partridge egg and it buries its excrement so it cannot be found. If found and someone drinks as much as a sesame-seed sized dollop in the morning, he is overcome by sleep, lays down deprived of his senses, and dies by sunset.

(35) There is a tree called the *parebon* which is the size of an olive tree and is only found in the royal gardens. It yields no flowers or fruit and has only fifteen roots which are thick

under the ground; its thickness is equal to that of an arm at its thinnest point. Wherever a span of this root is set, it snatches and attracts everything to itself – gold, silver, bronze, stones, and everything else except amber. If as much as a cubit of this root is placed somewhere, it attracts lambs and birds; they do most of their hunting in this manner. If you want to solidify up to a *chous* of water, you could do so with an obol of the root and the same goes for wine which you could hold in your hand like bees-wax and it dissolves the following day. This is given as a remedy for bowel irritation.

(36) There is a river flowing through India which is not very big but about two stades wide called the *Hyparchos* in Indian, which in Greek means 'bringing all good things'. This river carries down amber every year for thirty days. They say that there are trees in the mountains which hang over the water (there are streams in the mountains). When it is the season the tree produces droplets of sap just like the almond tree, pine, or any other tree, but it only produces them for thirty days each year. When this sap falls into the river, it solidifies. This tree is called the s*iptachora* in Indian which in Greek means 'sweet' or 'pleasant'. The Indians gather the amber from the river. The tree also produces fruit in clusters just like a grapevine and the berries are similar to the nuts from Pontus.

(37) According to Ctesias, in these mountains live men who have the head of a dog. Their clothes come from wild animals and they converse not with speech, but by barking like dogs, and this is how they understand each other. They have larger teeth than dogs and claws that are similar but longer and more rounded. They live in the mountains as far as the Indus River

and they are black and very just, like the rest of the Indians with whom they associate. Since they understand what the other Indians say but cannot converse, they communicate by barking and making gestures with their hands and fingers like the deaf and mute. The Indians call them *Kalystrioi* which in Greek means Cynocephaloi ('Dog-Headed People'). They have 120,000 people in their tribe.

(38) Near the source of the river grows a crimson blossom from which comes a purple dye as good as that of the Greeks but much brighter. (39) There are animals there the size of the scarab and red like cinnabar which have incredibly long feet and are soft like a worm. These creatures live in the trees which produce amber and they feast on their fruit. They also kill the tree just like the pests that destroy the vines in Greece. The Indians grind up these bugs and dye their red cloths, garments, and whatever else they wish. These are better in quality than the dyed garments of Persia.

(40) The Cynocephaloi who dwell in the mountains do not work but live off the wild game. They make a kill and then bake the meat in the sun. They raise sheep, goats, and asses and drink both fresh and sour milk from sheep. They eat the fruit off the *siptachora* tree (which is very sweet) from which amber is produced. They dry the fruit and put it in large baskets like the Greeks do with raisins. (41) The Cynocephaloi make rafts, load them with cargo of this fruit along with the purple dye purified from the flower, and 260 talents annually. This and the same amount of the substance used to make the red dye along with 1,000 talents of amber are sent each year to the king of the Indians. They gather more of it and sell it to

the Indians in exchange for bread, meal, and cotton garments. They also exchange the fruit for swords which they use to hunt wild game (they also use bows and spears, and they are very skilled with both). Because they inhabit lofty and inaccessible mountains they are unfamiliar with war. Every fifth year the king gives them a gift of 300,000 bows, the same number of javelins, 120,000 light shields, and 50,000 swords.

(42) The Cynocephaloi live not in houses but in caves. They hunt animals with bows and javelins and capture them by way of pursuit since they are fast runners. Their women bathe once per month when their menstrual cycle comes but at no other time. The men do not bathe but wash their hands, anoint their bodies three times per month with the oil from milk, and use hides to wipe themselves down. They do not wear shaggy clothes but very thin strips of leather and this is done by both the men and the women. Members of the wealthiest class wear clothes made of linen, but these men are few. They do not have beds but make mattresses of straw. The one who possesses the most sheep is considered to be the richest since the rest of their possessions are approximately of equal value. (43) All of them, both men and women, have a tail just above the rear end like that of a dog, only bigger and hairier. They fornicate with their women on all fours like dogs and it is shameful for them to do it any other way. They are just men who enjoy the greatest longevity of any people, for they live for 170 years and some of them even reach the age of 200.

(44) They say another race lives beyond these people past the source of the river. These men are dark like the rest of the Indians and do not work, eat grain, or drink water. Instead,

they tend many flocks of sheep, oxen, goats, and cattle and drink only milk and nothing else. When their young are born, they do not have an anus nor do they have bowel movements. They have buttocks but the orifice is grown together. Consequently, they do no pass excrement but they say their urine is like cheese, not thick but foul. They say that once they drink early in the morning and again in the middle of the day, they ingest a sweet root which does not allow milk to solidify in their abdomen. They gnaw on this root in the evening and vomit everything up with ease.

(45) There are wild asses in India the size of horses and even bigger. They have a white body, crimson head, and deep blue eyes. They have a horn in the middle of their brow one and a half cubits in length. The bottom part of the horn for as much as two palms towards the brow is bright white. The tip of the horn is sharp and deep vermillion in colour while the rest in the middle is black. They say that whoever drinks from the horn (which they fashion into cups) is immune to seizures and the holy sickness and suffers no effects from poison, whether they drink wine, water, or anything else from the cup either before or after ingesting the drug. He also says that other asses, both tame and wild, and the other solid-hoofed animals have no astragalos or bile in the liver. However, these creatures do have an astragalos and bile in the liver. The astragalos, which is similar in size and shape to that of an ox, is the most beautiful I have ever seen. It is as heavy as lead and the color of cinnabar even at its deepest points. This animal is extremely swift and strong and neither horse nor any other animal can overtake it in pursuit. It begins running

slowly, but the longer it runs, the more speed it picks up as it exerts itself brilliantly. Usually this animal cannot be hunted, but when they bring their young to pasture and are surrounded by many men on horseback, they choose not to flee and abandon their colts; rather, they fight both with their horn and by kicking and biting. They kill many horses and men, but they are taken down by the bow and javelin, as one could never capture them alive. Their flesh is inedible on account of its bitterness, but they are hunted for their horns and astragaloi.

(46) In the Indus River there is a worm that resembles the one that lives in the fig tree and is more or less seven cubits long. They say it is so wide that a ten-year-old child could hardly embrace it. It has two teeth, one up top and one below, and eats whatever it grabs with these teeth. Throughout the day they live in the mud of the river but come out by night. When it comes across an ox or camel on land, it bites it, then drags the beast into the river and consumes everything except the intestines. It is caught on a giant fishhook baited with a kid or a lamb and fixed to an iron chain. After catching one, they hang it up for thirty days and set a jar under it because thick oil drips from it enough to fill ten attic *kotylae*. When the thirty days have passed, they discard the worm, secure the oil, and bring it to the king of the Indians. The king is the only one to possess it, since it is not permitted for anyone else to have the oil from the worm. Whatever this oil is poured on, whether wood or living being, it becomes kindled and burns with a fire that can only be extinguished by a lot of thick clay.

(47) There is a tall tree in India which is similar to the cedar or cypress but with leaves like the date-palm only a little wider. It has no axil but blooms like the male laurel and bears no fruit. In Indian it is called the *karpion* and in Greek the 'scented rose'. It is a rare tree and droplets of oil drip from it which they wipe up with wool and wring out into containers made of stone. It is slightly red in colour, somewhat thick, but gives off the most pleasant of scents; they say its fragrance can be detected from a distance of up to five stades. It can be possessed only by the king and his relatives. The king of the Indians sent some to the Persian king and Ctesias claims to have personally seen it and said that he smelled a fragrance which defied description or comparison.

(48) Ctesias maintains that their cheese and wine are exceedingly sweet and that he personally tasted them and so knows from firsthand experience.

(49) He says that there is a spring in India with a perimeter of five *orgyia* and square in shape. The water is in the rock at a depth of up to three cubits, but the water itself is three *orgyia* deep. The most prominent of Indians, men, women, and children, bathe in the spring and jump in it feet first. When they jump into it, the water casts them back out. It not only repels men, but any other creature whether living or dead, is cast out onto dry land. This holds true for simply anything thrown into it except iron, silver, gold, and bronze; these items sink to the bottom. The water is very cold and sweet to drink. It makes a great noise like water boiling in a kettle and is used to clear up dull-white leprosy and mange. In Indian it is called the *Ballade* which in Greek means 'useful''.

(50) In the mountains of India where the reed grows, there is a tribe of men numbering 30,000. Their women give birth only once in their lifetime and their children have very beautiful teeth on both the upper and lower jaws. From birth each man and woman has white hair on their head and eyebrows for the first thirty years of their life. Their hair all over their body is white; after this it begins to turn black. When they reach the age of sixty, their hair is totally black. These men have up to eight fingers on each hand and likewise eight toes on each foot; the same goes for the women. They are very warlike and 5,000 of them serve the king of the Indians as archers and javelin men. According to Ctesias, they have ears big enough to cover their arms as far as the elbow and their entire back at the same time and one ear can touch the other.

(51) These are the stories Ctesias writes and asserts that they are completely truthful; adding that he personally saw some of the things he wrote about while others he heard from first-hand witnesses. He says that he omitted many other more incredible tales in order to not seem untrustworthy to those who have not seen them personally. These are some of the stories in his work.

F45a. Arrian *Anab*. 5.4.2 (Eust. Dion. Per. 1143):
According to Ctesias, if he is a credible source, the Indus River at its most narrow point is forty stades across, while it is a hundred stades across at its widest point, but most of the river is in between these two distances.

F45bα. Aelian *NA* 17.29

When the king of the Indians attacks an enemy, 120,000 war elephants are leading the charge. I hear that another 3,000 elephants of exceeding size and strength follow trained to attack and tear down the enemy walls on the king's order. They tear down the walls with their chest, according to Ctesias who claims that he wrote this after hearing it, and also that he had personally seen date-palms in Babylon uprooted and toppled by elephants in this same manner with extreme violence. However, they only do this on the orders of an Indian mahout.

F45bβ. Aelian *NA* 16.2 [L]

There are huge roosters that do not have a red comb like our native ones but instead have a colourful one like a crown of flowers. Their tail feathers are not protruding nor curved in a spiral, but are flat and they drag them around like the peacock whenever they do not hold them erect and stand them upright. The feathers of the Indian cock are gold and dark green like an emerald.

F45c. Tzetz. *Chil.* 7.738

If someone thinks that the reeds in Arabia defy belief, says Tzetzes, then who would believe Ctesias who writes that the reeds of India are 2,000 *orgyia* thick and that one of their knots makes two merchantmen?

F45dα. Arist. *HA* 2.1 p. 501a 24

None of these species has two rows of teeth. There is one such species, if we are to believe Ctesias, for he describes a beast in India called the martichora which has three rows of teeth on both jaws. It is the size of a lion and just as hairy with similar feet; however, its face and ears are human, it has light blue eyes, and it is the colour of cinnabar. It has a tail like that of the scorpion with a stinger at the tip and it shoots its stingers like a javelin. It makes a noise like a syrinx or salpinx. It can run as fast as a deer and is a savage man-eater.

F45dβ. Aelian *NA* 4.21 (Philes *De an. props.* 38)

There seems to be an Indian beast of irresistible strength which is the size of the largest lion, red in colour like cinnabar, and as hairy as a dog. In Indian it is called the martichora. It has a face that more closely resembles a man than a beast. It has three rows of teeth on its upper and lower jaws which are very sharp at their cutting edge and larger than a dog's. Its ears also appear human in shape, but they are larger and hairy. It has blue eyes which also look human. I think its feet and claws resemble a lion's. The stinger of a scorpion is attached to the tip of the tail which is a cubit long and has stingers on either side. The tip of the tail pricks its victim when close at hand and instantly kills him. If someone pursues it, then it discharges its stingers horizontally like arrows and can shoot them very far. When it unleashes its stingers toward the front its tail bends back, and when it aims them toward the rear it stretches its tail out flat like the Saka. Whatever it hits it kills, with the exception of elephants. The stingers used for shooting measure one foot in length and are as thick as a rope. Ctesias claims and maintains that the Indians corroborate this, that in place of the discharged stingers a new one grows as if it were the offspring of this dreadful item. As Ctesias himself says, it is especially fond of human flesh and it kills many. It does not lay in wait for one person, but chases after two or three and vanquishes all of them by itself. It prevails upon the rest of the animal kingdom, but could never overpower a lion. This animal takes great pleasure in having its fill of human flesh living up to its name, for the Indian name in Greek means 'man-eater' and is so-called from this habit. It is as swift as a deer and the Indians hunt their young before they develop a stinger and smash their tails with stones so they are never able to grow them. It emits a sound most closely resembling that of a salpinx. Ctesias claims to have seen one such creature which was brought to the Persian king as a gift, if he is a credible witness about these matters. However, when one hears of the peculiar characteristics of this animal, his attention is drawn to the Cnidian's history.

F45dγ. Paus. 9.21.4
In the account given by Ctesias there is a beast in India called the martichora by the Indians and the 'man-eater' by the Greeks which I take to refer to the tiger. It has three rows of teeth on each jaw and a stinger on the tip of its tail. It defends itself with these stingers in close combat and discharges them when fighting at a distance like a bowman's arrow. I think excessive fear for the beast has led the Indians to receive a false account from each other. (5) They were also deceived as to the colour of its skin. When the tiger appeared before them in the rays of the sun, they thought it was red and either

because of its speed or, if it were not running, its continuous twisting and turning, they could not see it up close.

F45dδ. Plin. *NH* 8.75
Ctesias writes that amongst these same men there is found an animal called the Mantichora which has three rows of teeth like a comb, the face and ears of a human, and bluish eyes. It is red in colour with the body of a lion and a tail with stingers like a scorpion. Its voice is as if the sounds of the pipe were mixed with a trumpet and it is a creature of great speed which avidly goes after human flesh.

F45eα. Antig. *Hist. mir.* 166 [F 107 XXXVIII Pf]
According to Callimachus, Ctesias writes in his history about the so-called immortal flame near the land of the Phaselitai on Mount Chimaera. If someone throws water on this fire, it burns brighter. However, if rubbish is thrown on it, then the fire is extinguished.

F45eβ. Plin. *NH* 2.236
Mount Chimaera burns in Phaselis and the flame is undying both by day and night. According to Ctesias, this fire is inflamed by water but is extinguished by earth or dung.

F45fα. Excerpt Const. *De an.* 2.67 (Suppl. Aristot. I 1 ed. Lambras p. 53.27)
In India dwell those called the Pygmies who possess a great tract of land in the middle of the region. The men are dark-skinned like the other Indians and speak the same language,

but they are extremely small with the tallest being two cubits while most, both men and women alike, are only one and a half cubits tall. Throughout their childhood they go around wearing cotton garments, but when they reach adolescence, they grow their hair long. The rest of the Pygmies have hair which reaches their knees and even longer while their beards exceed those of any other race. As a result, they say that, since they are small, they pull their beards down to their feet and their hair down their backs well below their knees. Because they grow their beard so long, they no longer wear cloaks but drape themselves in the front with the hair from their beard and in the back with the hair from their head. Then they gird their hair tightly around their entire body and so, in lieu of cloaks, they clothe themselves in their hair. They have very large penises which reach their ankles while they themselves are snub-nosed and deformed and look nothing like the rest of the Indians. Their women are small and ugly, just like the men. Their horses are like rams or a little bigger, their sheep are as small as lambs, and their asses, mules, and other livestock are no bigger than rams.

F45fβ. Ebd. 2. 556 (p. 139.27)
Amongst the Pygmies, just as they themselves are small, so are their sheep and other livestock.

F45fγ. Aelian *NA* 16.37 [L]
The so-called Psylloi in India (for there are others in Libya) have horses no greater than rams, and sheep which seem as small as lambs, while their asses, mules, oxen, and other livestock are similar in size.

F45g. Aelian *NA* 4.26

The Indians hunt hare and fox in the following way: they have no need of dogs when hunting, but they gather the young chicks of eagles, crows, and kites which they raise and train for the hunt. This is their method: they attach meat to a tame hare and domesticated fox, release them to run, send the birds after them on foot, and allow them to remove the meat. The birds pursue them with all their might and when they capture either a hare or a fox, they grip the meat and seize it as their prize. This is their bait and it is very enticing. Then, when they have perfected their skill in hunting, the Indians release them to hunt wild hare and fox. In the hopes of acquiring their accustomed meal, whenever they see one of these animals, they charge after it, quickly snatch it up, and return to their masters, according to Ctesias. In lieu of the meat hitherto fastened to the animals, the birds receive the innards of their prey as a meal. This is where we learned this practice.

F45h. Aelian *NH* 4.27

I hear that the griffin is an Indian animal with four feet with exceedingly strong talons which most closely resemble a lion's. They have plentiful feathers on their backs with black plumage but red in the front while their wings are white. Ctesias claims that the neck is adorned with deep blue feathers; the beak and head are like an eagle, similar to what an artisan would draw or mould, and its eyes are a fiery red. It makes its nest in the mountains but it is impossible to capture a full grown one; however, they can be taken into captivity when they are young. The Bactrians who are neighbours with the Indians say that the griffins guard the gold in that region and that they dig it out and weave their nests with it while the Indians gather what falls off. The Indians deny that these griffins are guardians of the aforementioned gold, for the griffins have no need of gold (in saying this I think they speak plausibly). However, when the Indians come to gather the gold, the griffins, in fear for their young, fight with the invaders. They contend with other animals whom they easily overpower, but they do not stand against lions or elephants. Fearing the might of these beasts, the natives do not retrieve this gold by day, but only do so at night, for they are more likely to go unnoticed at this time. This area where the griffins dwell and their gold is mined is frighteningly desolate. Those hunting the aforementioned material arrive in groups of one or two thousand, armed and carrying shovels and sacks. They watch for a moonless night before beginning to dig. If they escape the notice of the griffins the reward they reap is twofold, for they return home with both their load and their life. When those possessing the knowledge of the goldsmith have refined the gold, they acquire immense wealth in exchange for the aforementioned dangers, but if they are detected they are killed. They return home, as I have learned, after three or four years.

F45iα. Aelian *NA* 3.3
The sheep belonging to these men have tails a cubit wide, according to Ctesias.

F45iβ. Excerpt. Const. *De an.* 2.556 (Suppl. Aristot. I1 p. 139.13)

Ctesias says the Indians have sheep and goats which are larger than the biggest asses. For the most part, each ewe and goat produces up to six young, but neither bears less than three while most bear four. They have long and wide tails just reaching the ground, which they drag around; they are as much as a cubit in width. The Indians cut the tails from the breeding females because they cannot be mounted by the males unless their tails are removed. It is very sweet to eat and each tail has ten *minae* of fat while the smaller ones have only five. They make oil from this fat and often use it in their cooking. They tear open the tail of the male ass and remove three *minae* of fat or sometimes up to four. Then they sew it back up and restore it to health, for unless this is done, the ewes will not be able to carry around their tails. They do this every year as the fat grows back and the tail returns to its original condition.

F45iγ. Aelian *NA* 4.32 [L]:
The flocks of the Indians are something worthy to learn of. I hear that the goats and ewes are bigger than the largest asses and they bear four young each; neither the Indian goat nor the ewe would ever bear less than three. The tails of these sheep reach their feet and the goats have the very large tails that just touch the ground. The shepherds practise the custom of removing the tails of the ewes for breeding so they can be mounted. They also extract oil from the fat of these animals. They slash open the tails of the males, remove the fat, and stitch them back together. The cut heals back and every trace of it vanishes.

F45kα. Arist. *HA* 8.28 p. 606a8
According to Ctesias, although he is not entirely reliable, there are no swine in India, either wild or tame, but the bloodless and scaled beasts are all large.

F45kβ. Aelian *NA* 3.3
The peculiarities of the nature of these animals are as follows: Ctesias says there are neither wild nor tame pigs in India.

F45kγ. Excerpt. Const. *De an.* 2.572 (Suppl. Aristot. I1 p. 143.17)
Ctesias claims 'there are no swine in India either tame or wild. No Indian would ever eat the meat of swine anymore than he would that of a human'.

F45kδ. Aelian *NA* 16.37 [L]
They say that there are no swine in India either tame or wild. The Indians are disgusted at the prospect of eating this animal and they would never consume pork, just as they would never eat human flesh.

F45kε. Val. Max. *Facta et dicta memorabilia* 8 ext. 5 [L]
The Ethiopians make less astonishing claims about the longevity of this king, when, according to Herodotus, they say that he lived longer than 120 years; the same assertion is made about the Indians by Ctesias.

F45l. Aelian *NA* 4.36
The historians say that India is rich in drugs and suitable for

growing these plants. Some of these drugs are used to heal those on the verge of death from animal bites, since there are many in this region, and remove them from these dangers. Others are used to quickly cause death, such as the venom from the snake. This snake is a span in length and of a very deep crimson colour, but the head, as they describe it, is not crimson but white, not off-white, so to speak, but a white brighter than snow or milk. This snake has no teeth and is found in the hottest parts of India. It cannot bite and you could think that it is tame and gentle, but wherever it spits, so I hear, whether on a man or beast, each limb affected rots away. After capturing it, they hang it by its tail so its head is facing down towards the ground and then they place a bronze vessel under its mouth. The drops from its mouth pour into the vessel and this runoff thickens and congeals; if you saw it you would think it was sap from an almond tree. When the serpent dies they remove the vessel and replace it with another, likewise made of bronze. When the snake is dead, a wet discharge similar to water in consistency flows out. They allow this to happen for three days at which time this substance congeals. There is a difference in colour between the two substances; the latter is very dark while the former is the colour of amber. If you give anyone a sesame-seed sized droplet of this substance, simply putting it into wine or food, the person will first be seized with violent convulsions, then his eyes roll back, his brains melt down and pass out the nose, and he dies an agonizing but swift death. If you administer a smaller portion of the drug, death becomes inevitable but takes time. If you dispense even a sesame seed sized droplet of the dark substance which discharged from the dead serpent, it causes suppuration while consumption seizes the victim and he wastes away within a year. Many survive for two years dying gradually.

F45m. Aelian *NA* 4.41

There is a species of very small Indian birds which build their nests both amidst the lofty rocks and also the so-called smooth cliffs. The little bird is the size of a partridge egg and I think its colour is orange. The Indians call it *Dikairon* in their language, but the Greeks, as I hear it, call it *Dikaion*. If someone should ingest a speck of its dung placed in a drink, he would die by evening. The death is like sleep – very pleasant and free of pain – the sort the poets like to call 'limb-relaxing' and 'easy'. This death would bring freedom from pain and therefore is most pleasing for those in need of it. The Indians go to great lengths to acquire it, for they consider it the source of forgetfulness of troubles for its owner. The Indians also include this substance among their most precious gifts for the Persian king who receives it as a prize revered above all others; he hoards it as a remedy and antidote for incurable illness, if he should contract one. No one else in Persia possesses this substance except the king himself and his mother. Therefore, let us compare the drugs of India and Egypt and see which are more sought after. First of all, the Egyptian drug curbed and suppressed pain for one day whereas the Indian drug provided oblivion from ills for eternity. The one was a gift of a woman and the other came from a bird or some secret of nature which frees men from truly grievous bonds via the aforementioned agent. The

Indians are lucky enough to possess it so they can be freed from the imprisonment of this life whenever they wish.

F45nα. Apollon. *Hist. mir.* 17
According to Ctesias, there is a tree in India called the *parebon* which attracts whatever is brought near it including gold, silver, tin, bronze, and all other types of metal. It also draws in birds that fly close by. If the tree is taller, then it even attracts goats, sheep, and other animals of a similar size.

F45nβ. Hsch. s.v. πάρηβον
parebon: according to Ctesias it is a tree.

F45o. Plin. *NH* 37.39
Ctesias claims that there is a river in India called the Hypobarus which, as the name implies, brings all good things. It flows from the northern regions to the eastern part of the ocean near the mountains wooded with the amber-bearing trees. This tree is called the *psittachora* which means 'pleasant sweetness'.

F45oβ. Psellus ed. P. Maas [L]
(1) In India there flows a river two stades wide called the *spabaros* which in Greek means 'the bringer of all good things'. According to Ctesias, this river brings amber for thirty days each year. They say that a mountain looms over the river where there are large trees from which sap drops into the river causing it to solidify and become amber. This tree is called the *zetachora* which in Greek means 'sweet'. He claims that

the tree also bears fruit in bunches like grapes on the vine, but its berries are like the Pontic nut.

(2) Men dwell on the mountain who have the head of a dog but the rest of their body is human. They shout to the other Indians and communicate with them, but instead of talking they bark like dogs. They eat the fruit from these trees and the raw meat from wild animals which they hunt. They also keep many sheep and their teeth are larger than a dog's. They wear black garments made of hide and they drink milk from their sheep. All of them have tails, men and women alike, below the haunches just like a dog.

F45pα. Plin. *NH* 7.23
In many mountains there is a race of men with the head of a dog and clothed in animal skins. Instead of a voice they issue howls. They are armed for the hunt with talons and feast on birds. According to Ctesias, they numbered more than 120,000 at the time of his writing.

F45pβ. Tzetz. *Chil.* 7.713
Ctesias claims that there are amber-producing trees and dog-headed peoples in India. He maintains that they are very just and live by hunting.

F45pγ. Aelian *NA* 4.46
There are creatures in India the size of dung beetles which are red in colour. If you saw them for the first time you might liken them to cinnabar. They have very long legs and are soft to the touch. They live in the amber-producing trees and feed

on their fruit. The Indians capture these creatures, mash them up, and use them to dye their dark-red garments, chitons, and whatever else they wish to turn this colour and paint. Raiment of this sort was brought to the Persian king and their beauty was a source of amazement for the Persians. It was compared to the native Persian garments and amazingly was found to be far superior. According to Ctesias, this was because it was brighter and more noticeable than the revered Sardian robes. They are produced in the part of India where the dung beetles and Cynocephaloi live. These people get their name from the appearance and nature of their bodies. For the most part, they have a human figure and go around clothed in animal skins. They are just and do no wrong to anyone. Instead of talking they bark, but still they understand the Indian language. They feed on the flesh of wild animals which they capture with the greatest of ease, for they are very fast runners. They kill what they catch, break it up into pieces, and cook it with the heat of the sun instead of fire. They raise goats and sheep and, although they feed on the flesh of wild animals, they drink the milk from the domesticated animals they rear.

F45q. Aelian *NA* 4.52

I have heard that there are wild asses in India no smaller than horses which have a white body, a head which is almost crimson, and dark blue eyes. They have a horn on their brow one and a half cubits in length. The lower portion of the horn is white, the upper part is vermilion, and the middle is very dark. I hear that the Indians drink from these multicoloured horns, but not all the Indians, only the most powerful, and they pour gold around them at intervals as if they were adorning the beautiful arm of a statue with bracelets. They say that the one who drinks from this horn will never experience terminal illnesses. No longer would he suffer seizures or the so-called holy sickness nor could he be killed with poison. If he drank the poison first, he would vomit it up and return to health. It is believed that the other asses throughout the world, both tame and wild, and the rest of the other solid-hoofed animals do not have an astragalos in their ankle nor do they have bile in their liver. According to Ctesias, however, the one-horned Indian asses have astragaloi and are not lacking bile. They say their astragaloi are black and if someone should grind them up they would be the same on the inside. These creatures are not only faster than other asses, but horses and deer as well. They begin to run lightly, but gradually they run harder and to pursue one is, to put it poetically, to chase the intangible. When the female gives birth and guides her newborns about, the sires join them in the pasture and watch over their young. These asses are found on the most desolate plains in India. When the Indians set out to hunt them, the asses allow those that are still young and tender to graze behind them while they fight and charge the horsemen at close quarters and strike them with their horn. Such is their strength that nothing can endure their impact. Everything succumbs to them and gets pierced; however, if by chance it is crushed to pieces, it is rendered useless. They have attacked the sides of horses and ripped them open, disembowelling them. For that reason, the horsemen are too afraid to go near them because the price for getting too close is a horrible death for both themselves and the horses. The asses also have a deadly kick and their bite reaches such a depth that whatever is caught in its grip is completely torn away. You could not capture a full grown ass alive, but they are killed with javelins and arrows and when it is dead, the Indians remove the much revered horn from the animal. The flesh of the Indian ass is inedible because it is so bitter.

F45r. Aelian *NA* 5.3

This Indus River is without creatures, save only the worm they say inhabits it. In form it is similar to the worms born and reared in trees, but the ones in the river approach seven cubits in length, although you could find them bigger or smaller. Their width is such that a ten-year-old boy would hardly be able to embrace them. These creatures have one tooth on both the upper and lower jaw which are square and a *pygon* in length. Their teeth are so powerful that they easily crush whatever they grasp, whether it is a stone or an animal, either tame or wild. They spend the day below at the bottom of the river pleasantly dwelling in the mud and sediment where they remain hidden. By night they go forth onto land and whatever they come across, whether it is a horse, ox, or ass, they crush it, drag it into their own habitat, and eat it in the river; they devour every limb except the intestines. If hunger lays hold of them even in the daytime, then they creep upon camels or oxen as they drink from the riverbank, seize them by the tip of the lips, and in a violent rush drag them with a firm grip into the water and have their meal. Each animal is covered by skin two dactyls thick. The following way for hunting them

has been devised: they lower a thick, powerful hook fastened
to an iron chain rigged with a thick rope of white flax. They
then wrap both up in wool in order to keep the worm from
gnawing through them. Next, they bait the hook with either a
lamb or a kid and lower it into the water. Up to thirty men hold
the rigging ready to hurl javelins and armed with daggers
while sticks of very strong cherry wood are kept at hand
should it be necessary to club the worm. When the worm has
taken the bait and been hooked, they drag it out, kill the beast,
and then hang it in the heat of the sun for thirty days. Thick
oil is squeezed from it into a ceramic vessel and each worm
produces up to ten *kotylae*. This oil is sealed and brought to
the king of the Indians and no one else is allowed to possess
as much as a drop of it. The rest of the carcass is useless. The
oil has such power that if you wanted to burn up a heap of
wood and spread the embers, you could pour a *kotyla* of this
substance on it and kindle the flame without first putting a
spark to the wood. If you wanted to burn up a man or animal,
you could pour this on him and he is immediately consumed.
They say that the king of the Indians uses this oil to destroy
the cities that have become hostile. He does not wait for
battering-rams, penthouses, or any other siege engines since
he takes the cities by burning them to ashes. He fills the
earthenware vessels which contain as much as a *kotyla* each
and seals them at the top before hurling them at the gates.
When they hit the embrasures the vessels shatter upon impact
causing the oil to sink down and an unquenchable fire covers
over the doors. The fire burns their weapons and fighting
soldiers with its superior strength. However, it can be subdued

and extinguished with a large amount of rubbish poured over it. This is the account given by Ctesias of Cnidus.

F45sα. Antigon. *Hist. mir.* 150
[Callimachus] says that Ctesias writes about one of the lakes in India which does not receive anything thrown into it, like the lakes in Sicily and Media, except gold, iron, and bronze. If something falls into the lake horizontally, it expels the object upright and it cures the so-called white disease. On another lake oil floats on the surface on a calm day.

F45sβ. Paradox. Flor. 3
There is a spring in India which casts those who dive in back out onto dry land as if from a catapult, according to the history of Ctesias.

45t. Plin. *NH* 7.23 (F45p)
Amongst a certain Indian race the women give birth once in their life and their offspring are immediately grey-haired.

F46a. Aelian *NH* 16.31
Ctesias says in his account of India that the so-called Cynamolgoi, who are adamant dog-breeders, raise many dogs which are similar in size to those in Hyrcania. The Cnidian claims this is done because from the summer solstice to the middle of winter herds of cattle roam about as if a beehive or wasps' nest had been disturbed. The cattle are countless in number and are wild, violent creatures who vent their anger with their horns. They cannot remove these creatures in any

other way except to unleash their dogs which are well-bred and always trained for this purpose and so can easily contend with and overcome the cattle. They remove the parts of their flesh deemed suitable for consumption and dole out the rest to the dogs gladly sharing their fruits with their benefactors. During the season when the cattle no longer roam this region, these men use their dogs to hunt other species. They milk their bitches, from which act their name is derived, and drink it as we do with the milk of sheep and goats.

F46b. Pollux. 5.41
The Cynamolgoi are dogs who live around the southern marshes who take their nourishment from the milk of cows. They fight with the Indian cattle who attack the people during the summer, according to Ctesias.

F47a. Antigon. *Hist. mir.* 146 (F I 1'a)
[According to Ctesias] in India there is a spring called the Sila not even the lightest object thrown in floats, but everything sinks.

F47b. Plin. *NH* 31.21
Ctesias writes about a pond called the Side in India in which nothing floats and everything sinks.

F48a. Arist. *HA* 3.22 p. 523a26)
It is untrue what Ctesias writes about the sperm of elephants.

F48b. Arist. *De gen. an.* 2.2 p. 736a2

For Ctesias of Cnidus is clearly wrong on what he says about the sperm of elephants, for he says that it hardens when it dries and becomes similar to amber. This does not happen.

F49a. Arrian. *Ind.* 3.6
Ctesias of Cnidus says that the territory of India is equal to the size of the rest of Asia.

F49b. Strabo 15.1.12
While Ctesias says that India is no smaller than the rest of Asia.

F50. Athen. 10.45 p. 434 D (Eust. Hom. *Od.* s 3)
Ctesias claims that in India it is not permissible for the king to get drunk.

F51a. Plin. *NH* 7.23: (F45pα; F45t)
The same author (sc. Ctesias) writes that the race of men who are called the Monocoli have one leg but show amazing agility by jumping. These same men are also called the Sciapodes because when it is hot, they lay on the ground on their back and shade themselves with their feet. They inhabit a region not far from the Troglodytes. Turning again to the west from these people are those who lack necks and have eyes on their shoulders. (24) There are also satyrs in the mountains of the eastern part of India in the region of the so-called Catarcludi. Satyrs are extremely swift animals running sometimes on all fours and sometimes upright in imitation of a human. Because of their speed, they are never captured unless old or sick.

F51b. Tzetz. *Chil.* 7.621-41 (Kiesling 629-49)

There is a book by Scylax of Caryanda written about India which claims that there are men called the Sciapodes and the Otoliknoi. Of these the Sciapodes have very broad feet and at midday they drop to the ground, stretch their feet out above them, and give themselves shade. The Otoliknoi have huge ears which they use to cover themselves like an umbrella. This Scylax also writes numerous tales about the Monophthalmoi, the Henotiktontes, and countless other strange marvels. He speaks of them as if they were true and none of them fabricated. Since I have not seen any of it, I consider these tales to be lies. That they have some elements of truth is attested by the fact that many others claim to have seen such marvels and ones even more incredible in their lifetime. This list includes Ctesias, Iambulos, Isigonos, Rheginos, Alexander, Sotion, Agathosthenes, Antigonos, Edoxos, Hippostratos, and countless others, including Protagoras himself and even Ptolemy, Akestorides and other writers of prose some of whom I am personally familiar with and others I am not.

F52. Plin. *NH* 7.28 (Onesikritos 134 F11)

Crates of Pergamum calls the Indians who live beyond one hundred years the Gymnetae, but many call them the Macrobii. Ctesias describes a race of these people called the Pandarae situated in the valleys, who live for 200 years. In youth they have white hair but it turns black as they reach old age. (29) In contrast to these people, there are some neighbours of the Macrobii whose lives do not exceed forty years and whose women bear children only once. Agatharchides relates this same story and adds that they feed on locusts and are swift runners. Clitarchos gave them the name of the Mandi and Megasthenes names 365 of their villages. Their women gave birth at the age of seven and reach old age at forty.

Other Works

On the Tributes of Asia

F53. Athen. 2.74 p. 67 A (F38)

... he (sc. Ctesias) also recounts in his book *On the Tributes of Asia* all the preparations for the king's dinner although he never mentions pepper or vinegar.

F54. Athen. 10.59 p. 442 B

For example, Baiton, the surveyor of Alexander, in his work *The Stations of Alexander's March* and Amyntas in his *On Stations* say that the race of the Tapyroi are so fond of wine that they anoint themselves with it and nothing else. Ctesias makes the same assertions in his work *On the Tributes of Asia* and adds that they are very just.

Periodos (*Periegesis, Periploi*)

Book I

F55. Steph. Byz. s.v. Σίγγυνος

Singynos: An Egyptian city, according to what Ctesias says in his *Periploi*. The citizens are the Singynoi.

F56. Schol. Apoll. Rhod. 2.1015b

This Hieron is a mountain near the Tibarenoi in the territory of the Mossynoikoi and it extends as far as the Euxeinos River. Ctesias also mentions it in Book I of his *Periodoi* and Suidas in the second book of his work entitled the *Macrones*. More precisely, Agathon in his *Periplous of the Pontus* says that it extends one hundred stades from the Trapezon. Eirenaios says that Mnesimachos discusses it in Book I of his work *On the Scythians* but he is misinformed, for Mnesimachos mentions the Scythian region as being in Europe while Apollonius and his predecessors place it in Asia. There is a third Mt. Hieron in Thrace.

Book II

F57. Schol. Apoll. Rhod. 2.339-401

Here in the region of Kyrtais and the territory of the Amarantoi far from the mountains and the Kirkaian plain the Phasis whirlpool casts a wide stream into the sea: Amaranton is with a circumflex according to what Herodian says in his *General Prosody*. Amaranta is a city on the Pontus. He claims that the mountains of Colchis are the source of the Phasis River, but Hegesistratos of Ephesus is unaware of this and instead interprets the meadows of Phasis as 'amarantian' because they are full of blooms and unfading. Ctesias claims in Book II that the Amaranta Mountains are in Colchis while Eratosthenes contends that the Phasis flows from the mountains of Armenia through Colchis and into the sea.

F58. Steph. Byz. s.v. Τίριζα

Tiriza: a Paphlagonian city; the ethnic name is the Tirizoi. Ctesias calls them Tiribizanoi in Book II: 'from the region of the Odryssoi to the Tiribazanoi who live in Paphlagonia'.

Book III
F59. Steph. Byz. s.v. Κοσύτη
Cosyte: an Umbrian city, according to what Ctesias says in Book III of his *Periegesis*. The ethnic is Cosytaian just as Motyaios is the ethnic for an inhabitant of Motya, a city in Sicily.

Book unknown
F60. Harp. (Sud. S 601) s.v. Σκιάποδες
Sciapodes: Antiphon in his book *On Concord* claims that they are a Libyan tribe. Ctesias in his *Periplous of Asia* says, 'beyond this region are the Sciapodes who have very wide feet just like geese and when it is hot they fall on their backs, raise their legs, and shade themselves with their feet'.

Fragments of unknown works

F61a. Antigon. *Hist. mir.* 165
According to Callimachus, Ctesias says in his history about the water flowing from the rock in Armenia that it carries along black fish which kill whoever eats them.

F61b. Plin. *NH* 31.25
Ctesias says that in Armenia there is a spring full of black fish which immediately cause death when ingested.

F62. Harp. s.v. ὑποκυδέω
Hypokydeis: There are places covered in shoal water according to Deinarchos in his speech *Against Stephanos*. A

moist place is *hypokydes*, as is evident from Book III of Ctesias. Euphorion says, 'like a drenched meadow'. However, in some of the copies by the orator it is written '*hypokoiloi*'.

F63. Lyd. *De mens*. 4.14

The origin of pepper according to the ancients and Ctesias of Cnidus is as follows: there is a tribe in the region of Azume called the Bessudai who have very small and feeble bodies and big, unshaven heads with plain hair like the Indians. They live in underground caves and know how to maneuver on precipices on account of their familiarity with them. These men cut down and gather pepper from the short trees which grow along side the bushes. Maximus says, 'The plant first existed in India without thorns but was cultivated like the grapevine either up trees or upon a stake. It produces fruit in bunches like terebinth and has longish foliage like ivy. The plant begins to produce fruit after three years and dies after eight. Once it is picked, it turns black, not from being roasted but from being placed in the sun which is why the pepper that is picked and dried in the shade remains white.'

F64. Serv. *in Verg. Geor*. I.30

The island of Thule is in the Ocean between the northern and western regions beyond Britain, Spain and the Orkneys. On this island when the sun is in Cancer, it is said that day is continuous without night. From this island originate many other marvels that have been described by Ctesias and Diogenes among the Greeks, and by Sammonicus among the Romans.

F65. Scol. Bern.; Brev. Expos. Verg. *Geor.* I.482

'Eridanus, King of the rivers': it is called the Po. There is much dispute about the actual site of Heridanus. Eusebius thinks it is the Rhone because of its size; Ctesias claims it is in India, Choerilius places it in Germany saying it is where Phaethon perished, and Ion says it is in Achaia.

F66. Strabo 16.4.20

Some say that the Erythran Sea gets its name from the colour it shows due to reflection, whether it is from the sun being at its zenith or from the mountains which are red from being scorched; both suggestions are just a guess. Ctesias of Cnidus claims that a spring feeds into it which has very red water. Agatharchides, his fellow citizen, says that it was named by someone from Boxos, arguing that it was because a certain Persian named Erythras who first came to the island ... who established colonies both there and at other islands and along the coast; he named the sea after himself. Others reveal that Erythras was the son of Perseus and the leader of this region.

Medical treatises

F67. Gal. on Hipp. II 4.40 [T4]

They criticize Hippocrates for reinserting a dislocated hip on the grounds that it would immediately pop back out of socket. The first was Ctesias of Cnidus, his relative (for this man too was a member of the Asclepiads). After Ctesias, many others followed suit.

F68. Oreibas. *Collect. Med.* 8.8

The treatise of Ctesias on hellebore: 'In my father's time and my grandfather's time, no physician administered hellebore, for they did not understand how powerful it was nor did they know the correct dosage to give. If someone administered hellebore, he ordered the patient to draw up a will since he was going to be taking a serious risk. Many of those who took the drug choked to death while only a few survived. Now, however, it seems to be very safe.'

Fragments of doubtful authenticity

F69. Tzetz. *Chil.* 3.83-101

The Assyrian king Sesostris, who according to Diodorus was called Sesoosis, was the sole ruler of Assyria and the entire world. He yoked the kings of this region to his chariot and forced them to tow it around the way others do with horses, and he was called 'ruler of the universe' and 'god' by his contemporaries. One of these kings once reduced him to humility with a riddle on how unpredictable fortune is. While pulling the chariot, he watched the wheels, thus slowing down the pace. When Sesostris said, 'Why are you going so slowly along the road? Tell me quickly', the man replied, 'Because after seeing how the wheels are turning, I am not running.' Sesostris understood what this man revealed and reigned in his arrogance. He unyoked the men and in the future acted kindly and with restraint toward them all. Ctesias, Herodotus, Diodorus, Dion, Callisthenes, Simocatus, and others relate this story briefly while others give a more detailed account.

F70. Tzetz. *Chil*. 3.640-647

... and why do I tell you that Cyrus remembered the favour? There is a common Persian custom regarding ingratitude that everyone must repay a favour when he is able to do so, and they harshly rebuke and chastise those who do not. They view those guilty of ungratefulness as acting very impiously towards their fatherland, their family and God. Xenophon wrote a history of Cyrus while Ctesias and Herodotus wrote about the Persian custom.

F71. Tzetz. *Chil*. 8.985-92

Herodotus, Diodorus, Ctesias, and everyone else say that Arabia happens to be a blessed place and just like India, it is very sweet smelling and gives off aromas, for even the stones when crushed emit a scent. The men of that region find relaxation in the pleasant smell and they smoke certain bones and horns; they also do this to regain their strength.

F72. Antigon. *Hist. mir.* 116

The historiographer says that the Persian Arsames had teeth right from birth.

False fragments

On Mountains

F73. Plut. *De fluv*. 21.5 (= Stob. *Flor*. 4.36.20)

There is a stone called the *antipathes* ('remedy from suffering') produced on this site (sc. Mt. Teuthras) which, when rubbed with wine and administered to patients, alleviates the suffering from dull-white leprosy and leprosy, according to what Ctesias of Cnidus writes in Book II of his treatise *On Mountains*.

On Rivers

F74. Plut. *De fluv.* 19.2
In this river (sc. Alpheus) there is a plant called the *kenchritis* which closely resembles a vine. Doctors boil it down and administer it in a drink to patients who have lost their wits and deliver them from their madness, according to what Ctesias says in Book I of his treatise *On Rivers*.

Interpolations

F75. Prima interpolatio *cod. Monac. Gr.* 287 (Photius) [L]
The tales of Ctesias of Cnidus on the marvels of the world:
The Seres and the inhabitants of upper India are said to have an exceedingly large physique as some of them are found to be thirteen cubits tall, and they live for more than 200 years. On one portion of the Gaïtros River there are savage men with skin which most closely resembles a hippopotamus since it cannot be pierced by arrows. In India too they say that at the innermost region on an island in the sea there live men, who have very large tails, like those depicted on a satyr.

F76. Altera interpolatio *cod. Monac. Gr.* 287 (Photius) [L]
In Ethiopia there is a creature called the krokottas, commonly known as the dog-wolf. It has amazing power and they say it

mimics a human voice and calls men out by name during the night so that they approach the human voice. They attack in throngs and devour their prey. The animal has the strength of a lion, the swiftness of a horse, and the power of a bull, but it yields to iron. In Euboea in the land of Calchis the flocks of that region do not have bile, but their flesh is so bitter that not even dogs will eat them. They say that beyond the Maurousian Gates it rains during the summer but it grows very hot in the winter. In the region of Kyonia he says there is a spring which produces a stream of oil instead of water; this is why the natives use it to procure all of their sustenance. On the island called Metadrida, there is a spring situated near the sea which causes a very low ebb in the tide at midday and at midnight which leaves so many fish stranded on dry land, that the natives of that region cannot gather them all, but leave most of them behind and they rot on dry land.

Commentary

The *Indika*

F45. [Ctesias] says about the Indus River that it is forty stades wide at its narrowest point and two hundred at its widest: Cf. F45a; the width of the Indus River, by Ctesias' calculations, would have ranged from 7 to 35 km. The narrowest point of the lower Indus in modern times is at Sukkur in Pakistan where in 1932 the British completed a barrage across the river which had a length of nearly 1.6 km. The actual width of the river would be no more than twenty stades, but Ctesias' exaggerated claims may stem from an observation of the river when flooded beyond its banks (Arora 1996 pp. 20-1). During flood season (July-September) the river can be several miles wide, although in modern times embankments are often used to prevent flooding.

the Indians: It should be noted that the 'Indians' discussed by the early Greek authors were for the most part not within the realm of Sanskrit culture (Karttunen 1991 p. 83 n. 50). What the Greeks then called 'India' actually refers to the northwestern territory of the country around the Indus (from which the country gets its name) in mostly what is now Pakistan (Karttunen 1989 p. 7). The Greeks had no knowledge of the Indian sub-continent and viewed the Thar Desert as the edge of the world with only the Great Ocean beyond it.

the population of the Indians is nearly greater than the rest of the world combined: Herodotus (5.3) simply says that the Indians are the most populous nation on earth. While both authors are in agreement about the magnitude of the Indian population, Ctesias makes his assessment of the Indian population in a more emphatic and exaggerated manner than his predecessor. This passage offers a glimpse into the dramatic style of Ctesias' writing showing how he sought to entertain and amaze his audience.

the only animal to live in it: See note on F45 §46; cf. F45r; Hdt. (4.44) states more accurately that the Indus is the world's second largest producer of crocodiles. It has been proposed that Ctesias' worm is actually a fantastic interpretation of the crocodile or the gharial, however his description seems more to be of a serpent influenced by Indian beliefs (see note on §46). It is evident by his use of the term 'animal' (θηρίων) that Ctesias is not including fish in this statement but rather he is only referring to the lack of other types of ferocious beasts (Lenfant 2004 p. 171 n. 780).

no men live beyond India: The Greeks viewed India as the end of the inhabited world (Karttunen 1989 p. 157). Herodotus (3.98) also claims that India is the furthest east of any known nation and that to the east of them is nothing but dessert. The testimony of these authors seems to be geographically based on the Thar which lies to the east of the Indus in modern Pakistan and India (Lenfant 2004 pp. cxxxviii-cxxxix and p. 291 n. 781).

It does not rain but India is irrigated by the river: While
this statement was rightfully acknowledged as untrue by later
writers (Diod. 2.36.4-5; Arr. *Ind*. 6.4-5), attempts have been
made to discern its source. Lenfant (2004 p. 291 n. 782)
contends that this statement reflects observations of the Sind,
the region to the south and east of the Indus where the lack of
rain was noted by Aristobulous on the Alexander campaign
(Strab. 15.1.7). While this assertion is reasonable enough, she
equally acknowledges the possibility that Ctesias is simply
drawing a comparison between the Indus and the Nile based
on the statement of Herodotus (2.13) that the Nile valley was
irrigated by the river. Although she declines to discuss why
Ctesias would make such a comparison, she may be right on
both accounts. It is certainly plausible enough that Ctesias
heard of the intense draughts that plague the Sind region from
either Indian visitors to the court or Persian travellers who had
visited the region. Since we know Ctesias was familiar with
the works of Herodotus, his predecessor's accounts of the arid
conditions of the Nile would likely spring to mind upon
hearing these tales of a rainless India; thus he probably was
not simply following a *topos* modeled on the Nile valley but
drew the comparison himself.

a gemstone called *pantarba*: This stone has not been
identified with certainty. The gem also appears in the Photius'
epitomes of Heliodorus (cod. 73 p. 51a) and Philostratus (cod.
241 p. 326ab/327a; cf. Bigwood 1989 p. 314 and n. 55).
Philostratus (3.46) gives a vivid description of the stone
saying that, in addition to its magnetic properties to other
stones, it glows at night like fire and sparkles when in the

daylight. Veltheim (1797) suggested that this stone was based on some type of opal which emitted a rich display of colours after being submerged in water, but most subsequent scholars agree that there is not enough evidence to warrant a plausible proposal (Ball 1884 p. 231).

a Bactrian dealer: Bactrian merchants who lived on the fringes of the Achaemenid Empire and frequently came into contact with Indians form a major source for Ctesias (cf. F45h; see Introduction, pp. 21-7, for a full discussion on Ctesias' sources).

the wall-destroying elephants: Cf. F45bα; F1b §16.4 and note; F48a and b with note; Although eighteenth-century scholars often cited this comment as evidence for the unreliability of Ctesias, his description of the elephant was remarkably accurate (Karttunen 1980 p. 106). There is some evidence indicating that elephants were in fact used to tear down fortification walls, which were often made of wood (Megasthenes *FGrH* 715 F17, whose testimony is confirmed by archaeological finds in Page 1930 pp. 135-40). In the *Samgāmāvacarajātaka*, for example, there is a description of an elephant breaking apart the gates of Benares, and in the *Arthashāstra* elephants are used to attack fortresses. Despite his criticisms of Ctesias (see F48a and F48b), it is clear that even Aristotle used him extensively in his treatment of the elephant (659a2; cf. Scullard 1974 p. 37), much of which is accurate (see the excellent discussion of Bigwood 1993a). While it is clear that Ctesias gave a detailed description of the elephant (see the greater detail in F45bα), little of his account survives, probably because after the campaigns of Alexander and into the Roman period elephants ceased to be a source of amazement.

the small monkeys with tails four cubits in length: Cf. Megasth. *FGrH* 715 F21; F21b, although Megasthenes claims the monkeys are larger than the biggest dogs. These monkeys are most often equated with the langurs which still inhabit India today (Ball 1885 pp. 279-80; Lenfant 2004 p. 294 n. 786), where they are deemed sacred. In fact, the name 'langur' is derived from the Sanskrit word *lāngulin* meaning 'long tail' (Thapar 1997 p. 265). The gray langur (*Semnopithecus entellus*), also called the Hanuman langur (see Jerdon 1874 pp. 4-6) is seen as a descendant of Hanuman who, according to the *Sundara Kānda* (the fifth book of the *Rāmāyana*), was a monkey warrior who helped Rāma rescue his wife from Rāvana. He was captured by Rāvana and his tail was set on fire; the black face, hands and tale of the gray langur are said to be a testament to this event.

roosters of enormous size: cf. F45bβ and note.

a bird called the *bittakos*: Aristotle (*HA* 597b27) calls the bird a *psittake* (with the variant *sittake* also found in the mss.), and the forms *psittakos* and *sittakos* also occur in later works (Bigwood 1993a p. 541).

It has a crimson face ... like cinnabar: The text at this point is hopelessly corrupt. Clearly the phrase 'like cinnabar' cannot be used as a comparison for something dark blue, indicating something missing from the text. Numerous attempts have been made to solve the textual problems. Bähr (1824) deleted the ὡς, which in reference to an object rather than a person is unusual in Attic prose (Smyth n. 3003), as mistakenly inserted in anticipation of the following ὥσπερ. Müller (1844 following Bekker) argues for a lacuna in the text and inserts the phrase ***ἐρυθρὸν δὲ before τὸν τράχηλον. Bigwood (1993b p. 324) argues for the insertion of the phrase τὸν δὲ ὦμον ἐρυθρόν rendering the entire phrase 'is blue as far as its neck, but on its shoulder it is red like cinnabar'. In any case, I have chosen to conservatively follow the text despite my misgivings.

It can converse like a human: The species of parakeet being described here may be the plum-headed parakeet (*psittacula cyanocephala*). The male of the species has mostly green (of varying shades) plumage but has a red patch ('like cinnabar') on its upper wing, a narrow black collar that leads to a black stripe under the beak ('a black beard'). Its head is a deep red ('crimson face') tinged with purple on the lower cheek and back of the neck ('dark blue as far as the neck'). For a full discussion see Bigwood 1993b pp. 324-7. The accuracy with which Ctesias describes this bird indicates that he likely saw one in person. The fact the bird 'can speak Greek' was probably the result of it mimicking Ctesias himself. That it speaks 'Indian' may indicate that the bird was brought to the court by an Indian traveller, or perhaps a Persian or Bactrian merchant who had interacted with the Indians. As such, this passage provides valuable insight into the sources of Ctesias for the *Indika*. We know elsewhere that he had seen several Indians at the court, so he likely obtained some of his testimony directly from Indians (see the Introduction, p. 23, for a full discussion of Ctesias' sources).

There is a spring ...: Ctesias was fond of miraculous springs as no less than ten appear in his extent fragments. According to Herodotus (3.96), the Persian king melted down the tribute he received and stored it in clay jars. This has led to the assumption that Ctesias often takes Herodotus and reinvents the account according to his own imagination (Jacoby 1922 col. 2059; Lindegger 1982 p. 104 n. 5 simply draws the comparison with no comment). However, this does not appear to be the case since beyond the vessels themselves, there is very little in common between the two stories (Bigwood 1995 pp. 139-40). Perhaps Ctesias saw these vessels at the palaces in Persia and received a different explanation of their use and origins. The tradition may have originated from Nuristan on the southern slopes of the Hindu Kush mountains where there were accounts of lakes with magical properties which contained valuable items (Karttunen 1989 pp. 8-9 n. 18). On the gold of India see Wirth and von Hinüber 1985 pp. 1123-4, Vogelsang 1992 pp. 204-6.

a perimeter of sixteen cubits and a depth of one *orgyia*: *c.* 7-8 m in circumference and 1.8 m deep.

There is iron at the bottom: Iron replaced copper in metallurgy in northern India *c.* 1000 BCE (cf. *CHIn* vol. 1 p. 56, 112, 615). It was thus commonly employed by Ctesias' time (Bigwood 1995 p. 136).

Ctesias says two swords were fashioned and given to him: The Persian monarchs often gave daggers or swords as gifts, among other fine objects such as bracelets and jewellery, to their benefactors (Briant 2002 pp. 302-15). Mithridates received a Persian dagger (*'akinakēs'*) from Artaxerxes (F26

§15.2) and Artapates received one of gold from Cyrus the Younger for being a loyal sceptre-bearer (Xen. *Anab.* 1.8.29). Ctesias may have received this gift from Artaxerxes for his role at Cunaxa and from Parysatis for the services he rendered to Clearchos (Bigwood 1995 pp. 137-8).

ward off clouds, hail and typhoons: It was common practice in the East to ritually attempt to control the forces of nature (Frazer 1920 vol. 1 pp. 244-331; Bigwood 1995 pp. 138-9). Ctesias appears to be relating an actual ritual performed by the Persian king in an attempt to control the weather. Polyaenus (7.11.12) gives a similar account in which Darius I while on his Scythian campaign planted his sceptre in the ground as part of a ritual to cause rain since his army was destitute in a barren region (see the study of Calmeyer 1989 pp. 125-9). The king apparently acted as an intermediary between man and deity who sought to control the elements by fixing a royal symbol (sceptre or sword) into the ground (Briant 2002 pp. 239-40).

The dogs in India: These dogs were famous in antiquity and were kept in various parts of the Near East (Hdt. 1.192; see also 7.187 where we are told Xerxes took them with his army). Their size and courage are well attested in both Greek and Indian sources. There is a description in the *Rāmāyana* (2.64.21) of huge dogs with fangs like spears and the strength and courage of tigers. Comparisons such as this, although common, may have resulted in confusion for the Greeks leading Aristotle (*HA* 8.28 607a4; cf. *GA* 746a34) to claim that the Indian dog is a hybrid of a dog and a tiger (it is unclear if he is using a source other than Ctesias). However, there is evidence to support the assertion that these dogs fought with lions. Sopeithes, an Indian king, gave Alexander a gift of Indian dogs and demonstrated their prowess by having them fight a lion (Diod. 17.92). In Indian literature, the *Mācala* dogs of the Vidarbha country were said to have the ability to kill tigers (*JB* 2.442) and in the *Mahābhārata* (2.37.8) a pack of hunting dogs is seen attacking a sleeping lion. Even in the present day packs of dogs in India are known to chase tigers away from their kill and feed on their catch (Thapar 1997 p. 255). Although the Brahmans generally despised dogs, there is evidence in Indian literature showing that the dogs were kept and used as watchdogs and in hunting (*RV* 7.55.2-4; see also Xen. *Cyn.* 9.1, 10.1 although he may be describing a different breed of dog and one not necessarily of Indian origin – cf. Platt 1909 p. 242). On the Indian dog see Karttunen 1989 pp. 163-7; Chattopadhyay 1967.

There are large mountains ...: Although the epitome of Photius is meagre at this point, it seems clear that Ctesias equated these mountains with the Mt. Sardo mentioned below (§17; see also §33). This mountain has often been identified with the Sardonyx Mountains mentioned by Ptolemy (*Geog.* 7.1.20; cf. Herrmann 1920 col. 2496) seen as part of the Vindhyas (Lassen 1874 vol. 2 p. 653) or its parallel range the Satpura, both located in central India (McCrindle 1885 p. 77 followed by Herrmann). Extending from the Satpura towards the south are the Western Ghats which may be another possibility (acknowledged by Lassen op. cit. p. 653 n. 4). Since the major range of the Ghats is the Sahyadhri ('the benevolent mountains'), might Mt. Sardo be a corruption of this name? Recent scholarship, however, rejects the idea that Ptolemy and Ctesias are referring to the same mountain. Lindegger (1982 p. 105 n.1) locates Ctesias' Mt. Sardo in the Himalayas and Karttunen (1989 p. 84), who proceeds with caution, proposes the Aravalli near the Rajasthan desert in Northwest India. Although Karttunen's proposal would place the mountain in the region mostly associated with the *Indika*, it is impossible to conclusively solve its location (see also Lenfant 2002 pp. 298-9 n. 798).

It is very hot there ...: According to Herodotus (3.104), in India it is hotter in the morning than at midday. This perhaps comes from the belief that the Indians were located at the eastern end of the world and how a rising sun in the east appears larger than at midday.

the Greek Sea: i.e. the Aegean Sea. The sea in India referred to here is likely the Eastern Ocean which to the Greeks formed an eastern boundary of the world (Hecat. *FGrH* 1 F36) or what Herodotus referred to as the Red Sea (4.40). There is nothing in the fragments of the *Indika* to indicate that Ctesias encountered any travellers, Indian or otherwise, who had been far east enough to know of the Bay of Bengal. Perhaps this is a reference to the Arabian Sea into which the Indus flows in modern Pakistan.

four dactyls: *c.* 7 cm.

the so-called Indian reed: Cf. F1b §17.5 and F45c and note where we are told that one section between the nodes can make two boats; see also Megast. *FGrH* 715 F27b and Plin. *NH* 7.2.21 both of whom seem to be influenced by Ctesias, and Thphr. *HP* 4.11 also treats the subject. Various attempts have been made to identify this plant. Lassen (1874 vol. pp. 645-6) first proposed that the plant in question was a species of bamboo since it has nodes and can reach up to 35 m in height. Furthermore, many species have a hollow stem and are thus called 'female' while those with a solid stem are referred to as 'male' (cf. *WOI* p. 145; see also Lenfant 2004 p. 300 n. 804). Although Lassen's proposal is generally accepted, Ball (1885 pp. 335-6) suggested instead a species of the Palmyra palm since it has a much larger girth (six foot circumference at the base) than bamboo, one more fitting for constructing canoes. The tree, which is native to the Sind region, can also grow between 40-60 feet in height and up to 100 feet in some places. He also notes that the Sanskrit word for the Palmyra is *Trinarāja* meaning 'king of the reeds'. However, he fails to acknowledge the presence of nodes, which the Palmyra lacks and which are so prevalent in the sources (cf. Hdt. 3.98; Karttunen 1989 p. 189 n. 267). Furthermore, it is often overlooked that bamboo grows in clusters and it is possible that the reference to the girth of the reed originates from the girth of an entire cluster. Perhaps Ctesias' informant mistook a cluster for a single tree or, more likely, the confusion occurred in translation and Ctesias misunderstood his informant. While the extreme size of the reed accords well with the Greek view on the far reaches of the world, there may be eastern origins to this account since fantastic reeds also occur in Indian literature. In the *Mahābhārata* (2.48.2-4) and the *Rāmāyana* (4.42.37-8) along the banks of the Sila river (cf. F47a and note) on the boundary of the mythical land Uttarakuru, there grows the *kīcaka* reed which is the only thing that does not turn to stone when touched by the water. Thus, boats formed of this reed are the only means of crossing the river. Moreover, like the Ctesianic reed, the *kīcaka* is often identified as a species of hallow bamboo (Karttunen op. cit. pp. 188-9).

There lives in India a beast called the martichora: CF. F45dα-δ; Believed to be derived from OP *martiya-* ('man') and *x^{v}ār* ('consume') (Frisk 1960 p. 178; McCrindle 1881 p. 298 n. 25 gives *kordeh*). The Iranian root indicates that Ctesias likely received his information from a Persian source (Arora 1991 p. 90) or at least through a Persian interpreter (F45dβ seems to indicate an Indian source; perhaps the interpreter simply translated the phrase man-eater into Persian rather than give the exact Indian phrase). Since antiquity this creature has been identified with the tiger (cf. F45dγ). Although some have rejected this identification and seen the beast as pure fantasy (Lassen 1874 vol. 2 p. 652), most accept it as plausible (see for example Bigwood 1964 pp. 74-5). In fact, many of the attributes ascribed to the martichora can be discerned in the tiger. For instance, at the tip of the tail is a small dermal protrusion like a nail which is seen as the basis for the stinger of the martichora (although Ctesias would have seen one with the stinger already crushed – cf. F45dβ). The tiger's whiskers are seen by natives of India as harmful and are removed from tiger hides when hunted (they are also believed to endow someone with power over the opposite sex). Unlike ruminants and equines, the carnivorous molar of the tiger has three lobes thus giving rise to the belief that the martichora had three rows of teeth (Ball

1885 pp. 280-1). Ctesias likely accepted his informant's statement that it had a human face since this is a matter of opinion and we do not know how close he was able to get to the animal's cage (Karttunen 1991 p. 79). However, many aspects of the martichora are in fact rooted in pure fantasy since there is still no accounting for the martichora's ability to fire its stinger like an arrow and to create the shrill sounds of the trumpet. While Ctesias is most likely basing his description on what his informant told him, he may have supplemented what he did not understand by looking at some of the artistic images surrounding him at the Persian court where creatures were often depicted with features from several different animals (Jacoby 1922 col. 2038; Arora op. cit. proposes that he may have seen an image of the martichora on an Indian artifact). The Dragon of Marduk shown on the Gate of Ishtar at Babylon immediately comes to mind which has a red scaly body, serpent's head with horns, front feet of a feline and rear feet of a bird, and a scorpion's tail (see also Lenfant 2004 p. 302 n. 810 who likens it to the *chimaera*). In any case, while it is clear that the tiger forms the basis of the martichora, it evolved into a mythological creature common in medieval folklore continuing to the present day.

a *pletheron*: *c.* 30 m.

he also describes their customs and manners: Evidently Ctesias devoted a portion of his work on mundane aspects of India which were neglected by later authors who were often more interested in the fantastic. Despite what the fragments may indicate, the *Indika* was not merely a collection of marvels. Unfortunately for the modern scholar, Photius (and other excerpters) often ignored such ordinary discussions, or as here, relegated them to mere titles (Karttunen 1991 pp. 77-8). It is perhaps from this portion of the *Indika* that F50 derives.

where they honour Helios and Selene: The sun played a major role in the religions of India and was prominently featured in the *Rigveda* pertaining to various deities including Vishnu (*RV* 1.154) and personified at times as Mārtānda (*RV* 10.72.8) and Vivasvan (*RV* 10.14). The sun is primarily personified as Sūrya (*RV* 1.50) who, like his Greek counterpart, drives a chariot across the sky. However, there is no clear evidence for a cult to Sūrya (or any other solar deity) in Indian literature and the earliest definitive references to a sun cult date to the Kushan period (130 BCE-185 CE; cf. Karttunen 1989 pp. 220 and 222 n. 202), well after Ctesias. Still it is possible to conjecture that Ctesias was in fact telling the truth. The 'uninhabitable region' is most surely the Thar Desert. Near the Thar is Multan which later became a famous centre for the sun cult and is hailed as the original cult of the sun god in India (Karttunen op. cit. p. 220). Although there is no evidence to support a cult existing here during the fifth century BCE, it would be an amazing coincidence if Ctesias referred to a cult in a region where none existed in his time but would arise several centuries later. It is possible that the later cult was continuing or reviving an earlier tradition of worshipping the sun. However, it is equally possible that Ctesias is in fact referring to a cult of Iranian origin. Early sun worship in this region is attested by the discovery of fire altars and a sun disc at Balambat in Pakistan (Dani 1967) which date to the Achaemenid period. Moreover, in Nuristani mythology, the sun and moon are often coupled together as they are here (Karttunen op. cit. p. 223 n. 210). Unfortunately, due to the scant nature of the fragments and a lack of external evidence, any hypothesis for a factual basis of this cult will be mere conjecture (see also Lenfant 2004 pp. 303-5 who acknowledges the possibility of an authentic solar cult but contends Ctesias' view of sun worship is heavily influenced by Greek mythology).

Mt. Sardo: Likely the same mountain as the one mentioned in §11 (see note).

There are no thunder, lightning ...: Cf. §5; In fact there are thunderstorms and rain in India. The heavy wind is likely a reference to the monsoons. Hurricanes are still prevalent in India and were obviously of great concern to the Indians of the ancient world (cf. §9 on the sword which can ward off hurricanes).

The rising sun until midday stays cool ...: This is a complete contradiction of Herodotus (3.104) who claims that in India it is hottest in the morning when the sun is rising but then it cools in the afternoon.

Indians are not dark-skinned from the sun but by nature: Ctesias is rightly correcting Herodotus (2.22) who says of the Ethiopians that they are black because of the extreme heat in their region. Onesicritus (*FGrH* 134 F22 §24), perhaps influenced by Ctesias, later criticized Theodectes for believing the sun to be the cause of black skin. Ctesias also correctly points out that not all Indians are dark skinned (cf. Hdt. 3.101

who says all Indians were black, but he seems to refer only to the south portion of the country), giving credibility to his claim to have encountered Indians at the Persian court.

the fire flowing from Aetna ...: This account has been connected with the story of the brothers from Catana in Sicily, called Amphinomus and Anapias, who after an eruption of Aetna tried to carry their parents to safety. They were caught in the path of the lava flow but for their piety they were spared and the lava flowed around them. Since the story first appeared in Lycurgus (in *Leocr.* 95-6 who only tells of one son carrying his father to safety), it seems that Ctesias is giving the earliest account of this wondrous tale before it evolved into what became a well known story to the Greeks (see Holland 1926 for a full discussion).

In Zacynthus, there is a spring: Herodotus (4.195) confirms this statement and claims to have seen the lake personally (cf. Plin. *NH* 35.178).

In Naxos, there is a spring: Stephen of Byzantium (s.v. Νάξος), who may be following Ctesias, also testifies to this phenomenon. Philostratus (*Im.* 1.25) mentions a stream of wine in Andros but makes no mention of its sweetness (see also Plin. *NH* 31.2; D.Chr. *Orat.* 35.18 mentions rivers flowing with translucent wine, milk, honey and oil).

there is an unquenchable fire: The Eternal Flame in Olympos in Lycia is still a source of amazement for visitors to the area. The Flame exists along the Lycian Way in an area known as Chimera named for the mythical fire-breathing monster once believed to be the source of the fire from its underground lair. The fire is actually formed by natural gases seeping through the rocks which combust upon coming into contact with the air.

Pygmies: Cf. F45fα-γ; The Pygmies first appeared in Greek literature in Homer who described their battle with the cranes (*Il.* 3.3-7). Because Megasthenes (*FGrH* 715 F27a and b, F29) reiterated the Homeric story placing the action in India (he called the Pygmies the Trispithamoi 'those who are three spans long'), many scholars have assumed that he was following Ctesias who must have described a geranomachy himself and simply transposed a Greek story to India (cf. Lassen 1874 vol. 2 pp. 661-3 who contends that Ctesias did so after hearing an Indian parallel; Wittkower 1942 p. 160). However, nothing in the two extensive fragments on the Pygmies supports this assertion. If Ctesias did include a geranomachy in his account, Photius surely would have included it. It is clear that the Pygmies of Ctesias are not the same people as those mentioned by Homer since their only common attribute is their size. Perhaps upon hearing of this race of small people, Ctesias gave them a name familiar to the Greeks and Megasthenes, thinking they were the Homeric race, later included the famous description of their battle with the cranes (cf. the discussion of Karttunen 1989 p. 128-30). The Greeks used the term Pygmies (literally 'the size of a fist') to denote a dwarf (Arist. *Pr.* 892a12; Hdt. 3.37; at 2.32 he refrains from using the term Pygmy to describe the little people). Ctesias then may simply have been referring to a race of dwarfs without giving their tribal name (see F45fγ and note).

Various attempts have been made to identify an historical

basis for Ctesias' Pygmies. The suggestion of Bähr (1824 p. 40) that they referred to a species of monkey is completely unsubstantiated by the text since Ctesias makes clear that he is describing people (they speak Indian and share their customs, serve in the king's army and are just). Malte-Brun (1819 pp. 351-8) offers a slightly more plausible suggestion with the Ainu tribe from the Kuril Islands northeast of Japan who had full beards never shaving after a certain age. However, their location northeast of Japan is far too removed from the area of India described by Ctesias and it is highly doubtful he ever spoke to anyone who had come into contact with these people of the Far East. Similarly, Mund-Dopchie and Vanbaelen (1989 p. 215 n. 37) propose the inhabitants of the Andaman and Nicobar Islands in the Bay of Bengal who, located east of the Indian subcontinent, are likewise too far distant from the area in question. Without elaborating, Kumar (1974 p. 239) identifies them with the Gonda tribe of Madhya Pradesh near the Vindhya range who are of short stature. Moreover, like the Pygmies they raise cattle and their location in central India corresponds to Ctesias' statement that they lived 'in the middle of India'.

Their penises are so large that they reach their ankles: This conforms well to the Greek idea of monstrous beings where sizes tend to be extreme. The Pygmies are extremely small but still have very large penises. Thus nothing is moderate at the confines of the world.

Their sheep are like lambs ...: Cf. Arist. *Pr.* 892a on raising pygmy-sized animals.

They hunt hare and fox ... with ravens, kites, crows, and

Commentary

eagles: Cf. F45g and note where it is made clear that this is not a reference to the Pygmies but to the Indians in general; this is the earliest testimony of falconry in western literature. Its first attestation is in Mesopotamia where it was practised possibly as early as Sargon II (Salonen 1973 p. 184, 207). The absence of falconry in Xenophon's *Cynegeticus* suggests that it was no longer practised in the Achaemenid period. Oppenheim (1985 pp. 579-80) argues that the Persian official called the *ša ana muhhi issurī ša šarri* ('he who is in charge of the king's birds') oversaw the maintenance of the king's falcons rather than that of his poultry. However, since there is no other evidence that falconry was still practised in the Achaemenid period, this is a tenuous argument. If the king hunted with falcons we could hardly expect Ctesias to attribute the art to the Indians without mentioning that the Persian king employed the custom as well. The art may have been practiced in northwest India during the time of Ctesias (Karttunen 2008). A passage in Pānini (6.3.71) makes a possible reference to falconry (although Karttunen 1981 pp. 106-7 admits it is vague), which would indicate that it was known in this period (Karttunen 1989 pp. 160-3 for a full discussion of the Indian evidence). The accuracy of Ctesias' testimony strongly supports this contention (see note on F45g). The species of birds mentioned by Ctesias have raised some questions and it is surprising that he does not mention falcons or hawks while kites, although belonging to the same family as eagles and hawks (*Accipitridae*), have been deemed unfit for falconry (Karttunen 2008 p. 359). However, eagles are still used for hunting in Asia (Le Coq 1914). Pliny (*NH* 10.60.124) refers to the use of ravens in hunting and their similarity to crows should not exclude the possibility that attempts were made to use the latter as well. On falconry see the studies of Lindner (1973) and Vögele (1931).

800 stades: *c.* 142 km

they also use sesame oil: Oils of various types and fantastic properties are prevalent in the *Indika* (cf. §42, 46 nd 47; F45iα-γ; F45r). The Indians in fact used various types of oils for numerous applications. They used sesame and mustard oil in cooking (Auboyer 1965 p. 196; see also F45iβ), but sesame was (and continues to be) the most common type of oil used (Auboyer op. cit. p. 30; Ball 1885 pp. 340-1). They also used oils in the worship of *yakshas*, nature spirits, by rubbing oils on the trunks of their trees (Auboyer op. cit. p. 154). Certain tribes of India used oil for anointing themselves (cf. *Mbh* 8.30.15-18; see also §42 and §47) and they may have derived some medicinal benefit from it. The ancient Indian surgeon Sushruta (*Cikitsāsth* 24) speaks of the virtues of anointing oneself with oil.

they say the mines in Bactria are deeper: Bactrian merchants likely made up a large portion of Ctesias' sources, as seems to be the case here (see the Introduction, pp. 23-5, for a full discussion).

the Pactolus River: Located in modern Turkey, the river flows from Mt. Tmolos and through Sardis. It produced gold (Hdt. 5.101) which was mined and became the lifeblood of the Lydian economy (see Young 1972 who describes the unique qualities of the gold from this river; see also Ramage and Craddock 2000 for a thorough examination of Lydian gold which includes studies on its composition and refining). In later times the river was believed to have been depleted of this resource (Strab. 13.4.5; Plin. *NH* 33.66).

where the griffins live: Cf. 45h; The passage of the gold-guarding griffins bears a striking resemblance to Herodotus' description of the gold-digging ants (3.102-5; Ball 1885 pp. 281-2 identifies both the griffins and the ants with the Tibetan mastiff). However, gold-guarding griffins were not unknown to Herodotus, who relates an account of Aristeas of Proconnesus (on whom see the study of Bolton 1962) describing the gold-guarding griffins beyond the one-eyed Arimaspians (4.13 and 27; 3.116). However, it is doubtful that Ctesias is merely combining elements from several Herodotean anecdotes to fabricate a new legend (as Bolton op. cit. p. 65 suggests). Ctesias seems to be relating an Eastern tradition, one different from that which Herodotus gives. Herodotus tells us he obtained his information on the ants from Persians and it is impossible to ascertain the source of Aristeas since his work is lost. The reference to Bactria implies that Ctesias is using a Bactrian source (see the Introduction, pp. 23-5, on this matter).

Although in India the griffin appears to have been a late import from the Achaemenids or Hellenistic Greeks (Karttunen 1989 p. 177), it was well known in Mesopotamia (see the studies of Bisi 1964 and 1965) and Bactria (Sarianidi 1988 p. 1284-5) frequently appearing in iconography. The figures appeared either with lion-heads (Goldman 1960) or bird-heads with the former being far more common (Bisi 1964). Although Ctesias describes the bird-headed griffin that is more common to Greece and differing from the Achaemenid royal griffin which always had the head of a lion, he appears to have been influenced by Iranian traditions. Both his griffins and the Achaemenid royal griffins share the common trait of being guardians. Moreover, the motif of the gold-guarding creature appears in Iranian traditions in the form of the giant bird *Sēnmurv/Sīmurg* who guarded a treasure from its mountain lair (Schmidt 1980). Ctesias then may have been told of lion-headed griffins (bird-headed griffins are absent from Bactrian art in his time) and simply retold the story in Greek fashion and described the griffin to be more recognizable to his Greek audience (see note on F45h for influence of artistic representations on his description of the griffin).

The sheep and goats of the Indians: Cf. F45iα-γ; Although fat-tailed sheep are absent from Indian literature (Karttunen 1989 pp. 167-8), they are commonly found today in Western India, Pakistan and Afghanistan where they are called *dumba* (Wilson 1836 p. 46; Ball 1885 p. 286). The sheep inhabited Arabia early on (Hdt. 3.113), were depicted in Sumerian art as early as the fourth millennium (Anati 1968 p. 1), and may have been mentioned in the Old Testament (Leviticus 3:9, though the reference is vague). Since sheep, featuring prominently in the *Indika* (§42; see also §22), evidently played a vital role in the livelihood of the inhabitants of the Indus and northwest India, it is plausible that this breed of sheep had reached the Indus valley by Ctesias' day.

There is no swine: Cf. F45kα-δ; Hdt. 4.192 who makes the same statement about Libya. This statement is untrue since swine are well attested in Indian literature (e.g. *SB* 12.4.1.4) and even appear in a religious context since one of the avatars of Vishnu is a boar called the *Varāha-Avatāra*. Today certain parts of India have no wild boars and large segments of the population abhor the pig, even banning them from being raised in villages. However, in other regions pigs are kept and some Hindus eat wild boar (Ball 1885 p. 286 who also notes that fossil remains of pigs prove that they were not a later importation into the region). Ctesias may have misunderstood his informant or simply obtained false information.

The palms in India: The date palm (*Phoenix dactylifera*) is the most common palm in the Indus valley (Ball 1885 p. 336; see *WOI* s.v. 'Phoenix' for a full description). However, the large fruit of the tree indicates that the tree in question is likely the coconut palm (*Cocos nucifera* – see *WOI* s.v. 'Cocos'; cf. Lassen 1874 vol. 2 p. 645) which is common in the southern portion of the Indian subcontinent but found as far north as Bombay. It is possible that Ctesias may have seen the coconut first hand from a traveller since even today it remains an important trade commodity for the Indians.

there is a river of honey: The image of flowing honey is also found in Indian literature. The *Rāmāyana* (4.43.1-62) gives a vivid description of the mythical land Uttarakuru where flows milk and honey. The image of freely flowing honey was common in Eastern literature when describing a paradise (cf. the famous passage of *Exodus* 3:17). This accords well with Ctesias' utopian view of India and he may be simply following an Eastern *topos* to describe a blissful locale.

He speaks at length about the just nature of the Indians ...: Cf. note on §16.

The king uses this when he wants to discover the truth in allegations: The use of truth serum to force the guilty to confess is attested elsewhere. According to the fifth-century Chinese pilgrim Faxian, in Udyāna, a land in north Peshāwar west of the Indus in modern Pakistan, the inhabitants employed a truth serum when guilt was in doubt in order to force a confession from the guilty (Lassen 1874 vol. 2 p. 654). The practice may have appeared in Hindu sources as well (Kumar 1974 p. 240). According to Pliny (*NH* 24.102), certain Indians used the root of a plant called the *achaemenis* which when taken by day would cause the guilty to be tormented at night by vengeful deities. On the administration of justice by the Indian king see Auboyer 1965 p. 52.

The Indians do not suffer from headaches ...: It was a common *topos* to describe peoples at the fringes of the world or from an earlier age as experiencing extreme longevity and freedom from illness. According to Herodotus (3.23), the Ethiopians live up to 120 years (cf. F45ke; once again Ctesias is giving an account more exaggerated than his predecessor no doubt in attempt to impress his audience). Similar attributes were given to men remote in chronology as well as geography. Men of the mythical Golden Age who were earliest chronologically were likewise free from illness (Hes. *Op.* 92). Such concepts were also common in Eastern literature as testified by the story of *Genesis* where the first humans lived blissfully in Eden. Furthermore, the generations of Adam (*Gen.* 5) enjoyed extreme longevity living upwards of 900 years (see also the utopia described in the Book of Isaiah 65:17-25). In Hindu literature, the four Ages of Man as described by Hesiod have a parallel in the Four Yugas. In the *Krita Yuga*, also known as the *Satya Yuga*, which corresponds to Hesiod's Golden Age, men lived without disease, aging, evil, or even toil as the earth provided whatever bounty was needed (*MBh* 1.144). Ctesias differs from the rest of these accounts in the detail he gives regarding the illnesses, which should come as no surprise considering his profession as a physician (Tuplin 2004). However, the very specific nature of his list of diseases seems to imply the result of an enquiry rather than simply trying to one-up his predecessors and show off his knowledge of medicine. He never says that the Indians live free of disease, rather free of these specific diseases. Perhaps these were ailments which he frequently treated at the Persian court and asked his visitors from India what sort of remedies they had for them only to find out that they had no experience with these problems. If this is the case, then this passage provides valuable insight what Ctesias may have discussed with visitors to the court. It shows that he was not just interested in marvels and romantic tales. It also may shed light on some of the common ailments with which Persians were afflicted.

There lives in these parts a serpent: Cf. F45l; While this species of snake cannot be identified, the description given here, though perhaps not accurate, is not fantastic. The characteristics of this snake could be applied to several species of snake. Its small size (*c.* 22 cm in length) is similar to the highly venomous saw-scaled viper which inhabits the Thar Desert and grows to an average of 30 cm. The act of 'vomiting' its venom is also confirmed in several species of spitting cobras which are known to spit venom into the eyes of a predator. While no species of spitting cobra lives in India today, several species inhabit Indonesia and Malaysia (e.g. golden spitting cobra, *Naja sumatrana*) and Thailand (e.g. black and white spitting cobra, *Naja siamensis*). The assertion that Ctesias' snake has no teeth may stem from a misunderstanding from the fact that spitting snakes do not use fangs to inject their venom as most other snakes do.

When a sesame-seed size droplet of the poison ...: The precision Ctesias uses in discussing the manner of death caused by the poison again reflects his profession as a physician and may reflect the sort of enquiries he made to visitors at the Persian court (see note above).

There is a bird called the *dikairon*: Cf. F45m; This animal has been identified as the dung beetle (*Scaraboeus sacer*) and its dung pellets as *charas*, a hand-made resinous extract from *Cannabis sativa* (Ball 1885 pp. 310-11). The first part of this identification is difficult to accept since the dung beetle in no way resembles a bird and apart from burying its faeces, it shares no attributes with the *dikairon*. Moreover, Ball's attempt to connect the name to the Arabic word *zikairon* ('concealer') is a stretch. However, the identification of its excrement with *charas* has been accepted by many. Although at first glance opium would seem a better suggestion, the substance was not introduced into India until much later (Lassen 1874 vol. 2 p. 652). *Charas* is often found in small balls that could easily be mistaken for dung pellets. Moreover, the idea of being 'deprived of one's senses' and the euphoric feeling of 'forgetting one's troubles' (see F45m) are compatible with descriptions of *charas*, with the obvious exception that it does not cause death when ingested in small amounts. The same arguments could also be made for *bhang*, another derivative of the hemp plant, which is found in the form of small balls and consumed either by eating or diluted in a drink called *thandai* (Hasan 1975 pp. 240-2). However, although hemp was mentioned in India as early as the *Atharvaveda* (11.6.15), it was clearly employed as a talisman and for binding amulets (*AV* 2.4.1-6). There is no evidence that it was used as an intoxicant until the Islamic period (Flattery and Schwartz 1989 pp. 123-4). Moreover, hemp was commonly employed in medicine throughout the Middle East and Greece in the ancient world rendering such a belief impractical and proving that hemp products were by no means marvels from the edges of the world (Benet 1975 pp. 45-8). Becerra Romero (2007) most recently proposes that the substance in question was a masticant made from the areca nut (*Areca catechu*) and betel leaves (*Piper betle*). This concoction, called paan, is often used as a digestive aide and breath freshener and acts as a mild stimulant. Its localization to this region where it certainly was held in high regard would have made it an exotic commodity for the people of the Middle East. Ultimately, it is impossible to determine with any certainty the historical basis for this account. However, since the dung of the *dikairon* was given both to the Persian king and his mother (F45m), it is conceivable that Ctesias had seen the substance in its prepared form and was told a fanciful story about its origins and potency, possibly owed to a confusion of the facts, either on his own part or that of his source (Becerra Romera op. cit. pp. 269-70). His erroneous statement on the meaning of the name *dikairos* (F45m) further supports this view. See also James (1887) who connects this bird with the Dikaios bird that appears in the Sahidic Acts of Andrew and Paul.

There is a tree called the *parebon*: Cf. F45nα-β; Identified with the *pîpal* tree (*Ficus religiosa*) which though common in the tropical parts of India, is only grown in gardens in the northern part of the country. Its figs are very small and may have gone unnoticed. According to Ball (1884b), its roots are often visible at the ground's surface some distance from the trunk of the tree, although one wonders if he is confusing the *pîpal* with some other species of fig such as the Banyan (*Ficus benghalensis*), which is also sacred to Hindus, or the Indian Rubber (*Ficus elastica*), both of which have pronounced buttress roots. As the *pîpal* is sacred to the Hindus, idols and metal offerings are often placed around the trunk thus accounting for its 'magnetic' properties (a much more plausible explanation than Lassen 1874 vol. 2 p. 647 who argues that the root was used as a divining rod). Furthermore, the juice of the stem of the tree is often used to make birdlime in order to trap birds, thus enhancing the trees 'magnetic' properties. Finally, the seeds are said to be alterative while the leaves and shoots are used as a purgative (Ball 1885 pp. 336-7; *WOI* s.v.).

a span: *c*. 22 cm.

a cubit: *c*. 44 cm.

a *chous* of water: *c*. 3.25 litres.

This is given as a remedy for bowel irritation: See the Introduction, pp. 20-1, for Ctesias' predilection for medicine.

Commentary

two stades wide: *c.* 371 m.

the *Hyparchos*: Cf. F45o, F45oβ; Also called Hypobarus
(F45o) and Spabaros (F45ob). The latter form of the name is
most often accepted as the closest to the original
corresponding with the OP *Vispabara* ('bearing all things')
and possibly coming into Greek as Ὑσπάβαρος (Shulze 1924;
Karttunen 1989 p. 184 n. 227). It seems likely that either
Photius himself or a later editor of his text 'corrected' the
foreign name to the familiar Greek word for lieutenant
governor. Since the name has no corresponding Sanskrit term,
Ctesias likely heard a Persian translation of an Indian name
as occurred with the martichora (see note above; cf. Lassen
1874 vol. 2 p. 563; Johnston 1942 pp. 32-5).

The river was often identified with the Ganges (Lassen op.
cit. p. 563 and pp. 658-9; Kiessling 1916 col. 329-30; Johnston
op. cit.; but see the criticisms of such an identification by
Karttunnen 1989 pp. 83-4 and p. 184 n. 227) since it flows to
the east (F45oα). However, Schafer (1964 p. 499) identifies
the river as the *Drsadvāti*, a small tributary of the *Sarasvāti*
which according to Schafer was the most important river in
epic India. Levi (1904 p. 83 followed by Andre and Filiozat
1986 p. 370) proposes the Swat (called *Suvāstu* in Vedic
writings) that flows through Afghanistan.

the *siptachora*: Cf. F45o, F45oβ, F45pβ; Also called the
psitthachora (F45o) and the *zetachora* (F45oβ). The form of
the name given by Photius is preferable if one is to accept the
etymology of the name given by Tyschen (as cited in
McCrindle 1881 p. 301 n. 60 and Lassen 1874 vol. 2 p. 645
n. 1) who correlates the name to the Persian *shiftekhor*

'agreeable to eat' (for an analysis of the name see Johnston 1942 pp. 31-2; however, see Schmitt 2006 pp. 60-1 on the problems with such etymologies). Regarding its identification, Ball (1885 pp. 310 and 337-8) proposes that Ctesias' tree was based on the properties of two separate trees from the same region that were combined into one. He suggests that the *kusum* (*Schleichera trijuga* or *Schleichera oleosa*) which is a common producer of shellac (see note below), was confused with the *mahwa* (*Bassia latifolia*) whose dried flowers are used both as food and to distil into an alcoholic beverage. Lenfant (2004 p. 312 n. 854) gives the more plausible suggestion of the Indian jujube (*Zizyphus jujuba*) or the Indian fig (*Ficus indica*; both of these species were mentioned by Ball but for some reason left unexplored). Both species of trees produce shellac, host lac insects and produce fruit that is dried and eaten. However, another plausible candidate is the hitherto ignored Gular fig (*Ficus racemosa* or *Ficus glomerata*), which, like other figs, produces its edible fruit in clusters that are often eaten dehydrated (although seldom raw), produces latex and is a host of the Indian lac insect. Moreover, it is found throughout India often 'along the banks of streams and the sides of ravines' (*WOI* s.v. 'Ficus glomerata').

the amber: Since India does not produce any amber (McCrindle 1881 p. 301 n. 61), this substance has been identified with the shellac secreted by the Indian lac insects (see below) which often dwell on various species of trees (see Ball 1885 p. 309). Lassen (1874 pp. 644-5) suggests that it comes from gum exuding from the trees (see also Johnston 1942 pp. 30-1 who likens the substance to the Manna exuding from certain species of pine). Lassen's assertion can be corroborated by the latex emanating from various species of ficus (see above).

the nuts from Pontus: i.e. hazelnuts.

men who have the head of a dog: Cf. F45oβ, F45p α-γ; There are several earlier references to Cynocephaloi in Greek literature, however Ctesias gives the first detailed description of them. Hesiod (Fr. 40A, 44) refers to 'Half-dogs' but the reference is too vague to determine any relation to the Cynocephaloi, although the first-century BCE grammarian Simmias of Rhodes certainly equated the two (Fr. 1.9-13). Herodotus (4.191), possibly following Hecataeus, makes passing reference to Cynocephaloi living in Libya. However, he may have been relating an African account created to explain the dog-headed figures which appear on numerous rock engravings (Karttunen 1984 p. 34) or perhaps be describing monkeys (Marquart 1913 p. 203) since the term was soon after used for baboons (Ar. *Eq.* 415-16; Arist. *HA* 2.8.502a). In any case, they bear no relationship to the Cynocephaloi of India. A fragment of Aeschylus (apud Strab. 1.2.35) refers to Cynocephaloi (see also Strab. 16.4.14), but this may be a reference to the same Cynocephaloi of Herodotus. The Cynocephaloi of Ctesias can be corroborated with Indian sources. In several of the Purānas there is mention of *sunāmukha* corresponding to the Cynocephaloi (Karttunen 1989 pp. 181-2 who adds several citations to Lassen's original). Moreover, the *shvapāka*, a low caste of Indian society whose name means 'dog-cookers' have been associated with the Ctesianic Cynocephaloi (Wecker 1925 col.

26), however the derogatory nature of this term given to members of the lower class does not agree with Ctesias' positive description of the Cynocephaloi. There are also Chinese accounts referring to Dog-heads which, although of a later date, share some characteristics with Ctesias and the Indian accounts (Lindegger 1982 pp. 57-62). Various attempts have been made to identify this tribe of people. Shaefer (1964), who identifies them with the Kauravas, the heroic tribe found in the *Mahābhārata*, has found few adherents (see also Lévi 1904 p. 83 and Lindegger op. cit. p. 55 who both see them as Tibetan). Lassen (1874 pp. 659-61; followed by Wecker) more plausibly suggests that they were a tribe in the Himalayas of black aborigines of non-Aryan stock as evidenced by their foreign language (here referred to as 'barking'), black skin, and shepherding lifestyle (Karttunen 1989 p. 183; see also *Mhb* 8.8 on the keeping of sheep by peoples of northwest India). White (1991 pp. 28-9, 48-50, 71) argues against any identification suggesting instead that Ctesias was simply reporting Indian mythology as ethnography.

they communicate by barking and making gestures: Simmias of Rhodes (Fr. 1.9-13) similarly claims that the Cynocephaloi only bark for speech but that they can understand any human language. While certainly influenced by Ctesias, he calls them Half-dogs (ἡμικύνες), undoubtedly after Hesiod (Fr. 40A, 44). The Cynocephaloi's ability to comprehend speech and their inability to articulate it are further expressions of their dual nature. They are at once both human and animal, civilized and savage. They can communicate with each other and other Indians but fall short of full speech. Similarly, they do not fully cook their food but they do not eat it raw either. While they do not weave garments, they do not go about nude either. Yet, at the same time they are civilized enough to barter with the other Indians and engage in husbandry. They portray many elements of early, more primitive civilizations and may reflect Greek views of early man (Gera 2003 pp. 185-7; see also Romm 1992 pp. 78-80).

like the deaf and mute: This is one of only a few references to the use of signing by deaf people in the ancient world. Unfortunately, the evidence is insufficient to determine whether ancient Greeks employed true sign language or the deaf and mute merely used gestures to communicate. According to Aristotle (*HA* 536b), those who were born deaf were also mute since they lacked the modern means to teach the deaf to speak. While such people would have certainly developed a system of gestures in order to communicate, it would have been necessary for the deaf to interact with one another in order for a full sign language to develop. Such conditions may have existed in certain areas where a high frequency of deafness occurred, but it is unlikely if the Greeks would have differentiated between gesturing and true sign language. See the study of Edwards 1997 esp. pp. 34-5.

Kalystrioi: While this name does not appear to reflect any known Sanskrit or Iranian word, numerous attempts have been made to find its origin. Reese (1914 pp. 85-6 n.1) attempts to connect the name to *kalusha* (misprinted as *kaluta* – cf. Karttunen 1989 p. 184 n. 234) meaning 'unclean'. Shafer

(1964 pp. 499-500) sees a corruption of Kurukshetra, the kingdom described in the *Mahābhārata* belonging to the Kauravas whom he argues was the object of Ctesias' account, and *kukura*, the term for 'dog'. Lindegger (1982) connecting the name to the Kallatiai, the tribe of Indian cannibals mentioned by Herodotus (3.38), proposes both *kālīstrīya* (p. 53) meaning 'black women', and *kauleyasrita* (p. 108 n. 1) meaning 'dog-shaped'. Bannerjee (1920 p. 216) associates Kalystrioi with Kharostri, the writing system of the northwest territory of India well attested in the records of Ashoka the Great. The term Kharostri came to signify the barbarians whom Banerjee equates with Turks or Tibetans living in the regions of the Himalayas and Hindu Kush. Marquart (1913 pp. ccviii-ccix, followed by White 1991 p. 233 n. 11) sees the name as a transliteration of the OP **sa-dauxštr* from the Sanskrit *shva-duhitr* 'milker of dogs' (although this invented compound can also mean 'dog-daughter'). However, this last suggestion requires the unnecessary correction of the Greek text giving them the name Σαδύστριοι (On the Cynamolgoi see F46a and F46b).

crimson blossom: Identified with the *dhāvā* tree (also known as *Grislea tomentosa* or *Woodfordia fruticosa*) whose petals are used to make a red dye. The tree is native to Northwest India and Pakistan.

There are animals there the size of the Cantharus beetle: Most likely the lac insect (*Laccifer lacca*, formerly known as the *Coccus lacca*; cf. Ball 1885 p. 310). The lac insect is found on over 100 species of host plant throughout India where it is cultivated and exported for its dye. The host trees of the lac insect include *Ziziphus mauritiana, Ziziphus jujuba,* and various species of *Ficus* (cf. *WOI* s.v. 'Lac and Lac Insect'), including *Ficus glomerata* (see note above).

the pests that destroy the vines in Greece: Crop-destroying insects were a cause of serious concern for the Greeks who were known to rub bear fat on their vines to prevent infestation (cf. *Gp.* 5.30; see also Luc. *Ep. Sat.* 26; Gal. 6.572, 12.17, 14.290).

the king of the Indians: As Ctesias was writing before Chandragupta unified most of the subcontinent and founded the Maurya Empire (323 BCE), it is unclear which king he means when mentioning the 'king of the Indians' (although Shafer 1964 p. 501 considers this to be the Kuru kings who were the dominant power in the *Mahābhārata*). The northwestern part of the country was ruled by several smaller kingdoms called Janapadas (or Mahājanapadas in Buddhist texts such as the *Anguttara Nikāya*). The two Janapadas in the northwest part of the country known as Uttarapatha were the Kambujas and Gandhāras (see for example *P* 4.1.168-75) both of whom were allies of the Kurus in the epic war of the *Mahābhārata*. As both kingdoms were contemporary to Ctesias and possibly vassals under Achaemenid authority who could have sent emissaries to the court, either one could be his 'king of the Indians'.

cotton garments: Ctesias actually uses the term 'garments made from trees'. The clothes of the fifth-century Greeks were made of wool and linen while cotton was confined to the East. The Greeks seem to have viewed such fabrics made from trees with wonder (cf. Hdt. 3.106). Ctesias also informs us that the Pygmies wore such fabrics.

they are fast runners: Cf. *Persika* F12 where the Choramnaians hunt in similar fashion.

anoint their bodies three times per month with the oil from milk: Likely a reference to ghee, which is clarified butter (Henry 1947 p. 99 n. 37). According to the *Laws of Manu* (2.29; 3.274; 5.37 etc.), it is often used in sacred Indian rituals (Lindegger 1982 p. 111 n. 1 on the use of butter by the Tibetans).

They fornicate with their women on all fours like dogs: The idea of copulating *a tergo* ('like dogs') was not a source of amazement for the Greeks who regularly employed such positions (See Kilmer 1993 passim). Rather the source of amazement for them is that the Cynocephaloi only fornicate in this manner and do so outdoors which gives them yet another canine characteristic.

They are just men who enjoy the greatest longevity: Cf. §32 and note.

another race lives beyond these people: Cf. F46, F46b and note.

drink only milk: The *Mahābhārata* (8.30) describes people in the northwest region of the country who, having obscene customs, drank all types of milk and ate impure food from foul containers ('licked by dogs'). Such stories likely formed the basis for Ctesias' account.

There are wild asses in India ...: Cf. F45q; Ctesias gives the earliest western account of the unicorn (Shepard 1930 pp. 26-33) and his description has continued to influence artists' renditions of the mythical beast up to the present day. Several elements of Ctesias' description, including the alexipharmic powers of the horn (see note on pp. 132-3), indicate an Eastern origin for his account (Karttunen; 1989 pp. 168-79; Briggs

1931). Although Herodotus (4.191) mentions horned asses living in western Libya, his use of the plural (κέρεα) indicates they were not unicorns. Persian wild asses (*Equus hemionus onager*) were common in central Asia in antiquity (now endangered) as is reflected in their literature (see below). In India, there is another sub-species of the wild ass known as the khur (*Equus hemionus khur*) which was common to Northwestern India, Pakistan and into central Asia (now endangered; cf. Prater 1965 pp. 227-8; Groves 1974 pp. 101-6) while on the Tibetan Plateau there lives the largest of the wild asses known as the kiang (*Equus kiang*; Groves op. cit. pp. 86-96), which until recently was considered a sub-species of the wild Asian ass (Groves and Mazák 1967). Although several suggestions have been made as to the origin of this creature, it is generally accepted that the Indian rhinoceros (*Rhinoceros unicornis*) forms the basis for the unicorn of Ctesias (Ball 1885 p. 284-5; Lassen 1874 vol. 2 pp. 650-2; Karttunen op. cit.; Briggs op. cit., and others; doubted by McCrindle 1881 p. 303 n. 74). Although now mostly found in northeast India up to Nepal (Jerdon 1874 p. 233), rhinoceroses once inhabited the northwest from the Himalayas to Peshāwar. As late as the sixteenth century (1519), Babar hunted rhinos near the Indus (quoted in Briggs op. cit. p. 279). While certain aspects of Ctesias' account can certainly be traced to the rhinoceros (see below), the unicorn is not merely a fantastic distortion of that animal. The proposal of Shepard (op. cit.) that Ctesias is relating an account based on a confusion of the characteristics of the Indian rhinoceros with those of the wild ass and of the Tibetan antelope (*Pantholops hodgsoni*) has won few adherents (although Trotter 1908 suggests that the animal is based on an Indian antelope called the Nilgai, *Boselaphus tragocamelus*). However, there is some plausibility to this since rhinos are not known to bite or kick when fighting as asses and antelopes do. Moreover, identification with the antelope may have support in Indian literature.

Ultimately, Ctesias' unicorn may not be based on an actual animal but rooted in Mesopotamian traditions. The unicorn has a long tradition in eastern literature, especially in Hindu and Buddhist traditions. The *Mahābhārata* gives one of the earliest accounts of the legend of Rishyasringa, an anthropomorphic unicorn ('having the horn of an antelope') who, as the son of the ascetic Vibhāndaka and a doe, had a horn on his head (3.110-13; see also Rāmāyana 1.9-11). In Buddhist literature he is referred to as Ekashringa – 'unicorn' (Mahāvastu 141-52). However, Iranian traditions more closely correlate to Ctesias' unicorn. The description of the unicorn as an ass reflects the Iranian origins of Ctesias' account, as the ass was a very important creature in Iranian literature. The *Iranian Bundahishn* (24.D) tells of the Three-legged Ass which lives in the Ocean Frāxwkard that has one horn, a dark-blue head and a white body (see Panaino 2001 pp. 162-7 for other accounts of the Three-legged Ass). Enkidu, the companion of Gilgamesh, is said in the Babylonian version of the text to have been the son of a gazelle and a wild ass (Tab. 8.3-4; cf. Tab. 8.49-50 where Enkidu himself is referred to as a 'wild ass of the hills'). More significantly, *Yasna* 42 of the Avesta gives reference to the honours paid to the 'pious ass' (translated as 'unicorn' by Mills and certainly associated with the unicorn in later Zoroastrian writings), which stands in the Vourukasha Sea.

They have a white body ...: The fantastic colours are very similar to those of the Three-legged Ass described in the *Iranian Bundahishn* (24.D; see note above) and directly correspond to the sacred colors of the Ch'i-Lin, a Chinese hybrid creature with one horn that first appeared in the second millennium BCE (Gotfredsen 1999 pp. 12, 20); but they have troubled scholars who see the rhinoceros as the basis for the unicorn. Ball (1885 p. 285) suggests that Ctesias is describing a domesticated rhino which was whitewashed and its head painted with cosmetic pigments in order to take part in some pageant or event, as the Indians still do today with elephants. Shepard (1931 pp. 28-30) offers the more plausible suggestion that Ctesias' description was influenced by a work of art. The exportation of dyed fragments is indicated elsewhere in the *Indika* (e.g. §39) so the hypothesis that Ctesias may have seen an Indian garment with a colourful depiction of a unicorn is conceivable (see also the view of Eastman 1906 p. 195 that Ctesias was looking at animal reliefs of a ruminant in profile on the palace walls at Persepolis; cf. Briggs 1931 pp. 276-7 on the representations of unicorns in Mesopotamia). Regarding the horn, Ctesias may still be describing an image seen on a work of art or he may have seen firsthand a cup fashioned from a rhinoceros horn painted with three bands of colours (see note below) since we know he had seen an astragalos from the same animal. After seeing such colourful creatures as the parrot (§8 and note), one can see how Ctesias

would readily accept that there were other animals similarly
coloured with brilliant hues in this remote land.

one and a half cubits in length: *c*. 66 cm; for the reading cf.
F45q.

whoever drinks from the horn ...: Cf. Philostr. *VA* 3.2. The
pharmacological benefits of the horn have a long tradition in
the East (Einhorn 1976 pp. 244-7; Karttunen 1989 pp. 168-
9). The Three-legged Ass of Zoroastrian traditions purifies
waters against the contamination of 'noxious creatures'
(*Iranian Bundahishn* 24.D.15; cf. Shepard 1930 p. 212). The
Atharvaveda (3.7) describes the healing powers of the horn of
the gazelle against the disease called *kshetria* when water is
imbibed from it (Panaino 2001 p. 168). The unicorn's ability
to use its horn for purifying water against poison is attested
in later traditions such as Codex B of the *Physiologus*
(Sbordone 1936 p. 321) and the travels of Johannis Witte de
Hese (Shepard op. cit. p. 213; Einhorn 1976 p. 242; Panaino
op. cit. p. 170). In the Cyranides (2.34), the horn of the
rhinoceros possesses similar powers where it is used to chase
away demons. Such traditions have endured into the modern
period, much to the detriment of the rhinoceros population, as
cups fashioned from rhinoceros horns have a long history of
medicinal use. They were employed in China for medicinal
purposes probably even before Ctesias' time (Shepard op. cit.
p. 28; Laufer 1914 p. 75). While there is no evidence that the
ancient Indians themselves used the horn medicinally
(although Philostr. *VA* 3.2.1 says that the Indian kings drank
from such cups as protection against poison, but he is likely
just reinterpreting Ctesias), natives of India as recent as the

nineteenth century drank from such cups as an antidote to poison (Ball 1885 p. 285). By the sixteenth century, rhinoceros horns were sought after in Europe as a preventative to disease (Briggs 1931 p. 277).

the holy sickness: The Greek term for epilepsy.

The astragalos: i.e. the huckle-bone. Ctesias' statement regarding the lack of astragaloi in solid-hoofed animals is incorrect. It seems that Ctesias had seen a specimen which was painted red and weighted to be used as an amulet or decorative ornament (Ball 1885 p. 285). Although its exact function is unknown, Ctesias clearly stresses the importance of the object. In the west the astragalos was used to make dice, which perhaps is why Aelian (F45q) claims they were black (Shepard 1931 pp. 35-6).

they are taken down by the bow and javelin: The hunt of the unicorn became a favourite scene in medieval art (e.g. the Verteuil Tapestries depicting *The Hunt of the Unicorn*). Scenes frequently depicted the unicorn being surrounded by men armed with spears who are often shown wounding the creature while it is being soothed by the maiden (see for example the illustration in the Ashmole Bestiary – MS. Ashmole 1511, fol.14v). Such images of the unicorn being hunted with the spear may have originated with Ctesias, but certainly developed into a Christian allegory with the animal being pierced in the side and dying in the maiden's arm, reminiscent of the *Pietà* (Gotfredsen 1999 pp. 57-9). However, other images, such as the engravings of Jean Duvet and *The Unicorn Defends Himself* in the Verteuil Tapestries (see Fig. 1) depict scenes which are more reminiscent of Ctesias' account. The former shows a unicorn violently defending itself wounding one hunter with its horn while all around are strewn wounded men and horses. Similarly, the latter portrays a unicorn surrounded by men armed with spears and hounds using its horn to pierce one of the dogs while kicking with its hind legs at one of the hunters.

Fig. 1. *The Unicorn Defends Himself,* Verteuil Tapestries (*c.* 1495-1505), reproduced by permission of the Metropolitan Museum of Art, New York.

one could never capture them alive: According to later traditions, the unicorn, a wild and ill-tempered beast, can only be calmed by a maiden. Hunters would place maidens in the woods to attract and assuage the unicorn at which point it was brought to the palace (*Physiologus* 22) or bound in chains (*Physiologus* Codex B in Sbordone 1936 p. 321; see also *Cyranides* 2.34). The theme of the beast being seduced and tamed bears a striking resemblance to the fate of Enkidu, who was wild and lived amongst the animals before being seduced by a prostitute after which he becomes more 'civilized'. If these two traditions are connected (see Panaino 2001), then it is telling that by the Christian period the prostitute has been replaced by the virgin, a representation of Mary. The presence of the maiden would dominate medieval accounts of the unicorn (see for example the famous *The Lady and The Unicorn Tapestries*; cf. Gotfredsen 1999 pp. 45-50, 90-103). In any case, it is important to note that this tradition of the maiden was not prevalent in the time of Ctesias (cf. Ael. *HA* 16.20 likely derived from Megasthenes).

Their flesh is inedible on account of its bitterness: The flesh of the rhinoceros was used by the Indians in rituals. According to Manu (3.272), the flesh is offered to the Manes and produces satisfaction for endless time (Briggs 1931 p. 289). It is possible that the Indians offered food they found inedible to the gods in the same way as the Greeks offered bones and fat in reference to the Prometheus myth. Its meat was used medicinally to ward off cough, promote long life and help the liver (Karttunen 1989 p. 169).

there is a worm ...: Cf. §3 and note; often identified with the crocodile (Bähr 1824 p. 335; Ball 1885 pp. 306-8). While the eating habits of the creature described as well as the methods of catching it accurately correlate to the crocodile, this hypothesis is unlikely since the Greeks had long been familiar with it (Hdt. 4.44). Amigues (2007) has suggested that the factual basis for the fantastic worm is instead an amalgamation of the gavial (*Gavialis gangeticus*) and the marsh crocodile (*Crocodilus palustris*). Nevertheless, the Indus worm, which is clearly of a serpentine nature, hardly resembles a crocodile or a gavial. Furthermore, there is no sound explanation for the poison produced by the worm if either is meant (Ball's identification of the substance with petroleum from the Punjab is unconvincing). The source of Ctesias' worm may instead lay in the realm of Indian mythology rather than zoology since the worship of snakes was of particular importance in the northwest (Lassen 1874 vol. 2 p. 647). Nāgas were a race of supernatural beings usually depicted as snakes who were capable of issuing forth a blast of fire from their nostrils (e.g. *J* vol. III n. 386; see the study of Vogel 1926 p. 15 and passim). Shesha, the king of the Nāgas who is said to have held the world (*Mhb* 1.36) and who often appears as the *avatāra* Balarāma (*Bhag-P* 10.1.24), is described as a white serpent. Philostratus (*VA* 3.1), who is clearly following Ctesias (Reese 1914 pp. 90-1), describes the Indus worm as white. Moreover, in the *Harivamsha-Purāna*, Shesha is seen hanging from a tree with *kālakūta* poison flowing from its mouth which burns the earth. Thus, it is quite plausible that the Indus worm is in fact Shesha and Ctesias is relating a tradition from the northwest now lost (Karttunen 1989 pp. 190-2). A tradition of Shesha localized to the northwest would also explain the depiction of the worm as an aquatic animal with the attributes of the crocodile ascribed to it since the latter was a much feared beast in those parts.

seven cubits: *c*. 3.25 m.

ten attic *kotylae*: *c*. 2.7 litres.

the *karpion*: McCrindle (1881 p. 303 n. 81) connects this term to the Tamil-Malayām word *karrupu* or *kārppu* used to describe cinnamon oil. He identifies them both with the Sanskrit term for camphor, *karpūra* (Lassen 1874 vol. 2 pp. 564-6 who also identifies the substance as cinnamon oil). Camphor is obtained from a species of laurel (*Cinnamomum camphora*). This hypothesis is made even more plausible by the fact that some forms of *C. camphora* do not produce camphor but only an aromatic oil, such as that described by Ctesias (*WOI* s.v. 'cinnamomum'). However, this tree was not found in India in Ctesias' time, although about 20 species of *C. camphora* are now grown in various parts of India which were introduced from the Far East. It is possible, though unlikely, that a vial of camphor oil reached Ctesias from the Far East. Ball (1885 p. 339) plausibly contends that Ctesias, or his source, has combined the characteristics of a species of laurel (*Laurus cinnamomum* or *Cinnamomum verum*) with those of the screw pine (*Pandanus odoratissimus*). The latter species more closely corresponds to the palm-like characteristics of the *karpion* and its leaves are distilled to create a perfume called *keorā*.

five stades: *c*. 877 m.

their cheese and wine: While the grapevine was not introduced to the Indian subcontinent until much later, grapes were cultivated in the northwest region since antiquity. Greek sources speak of a cult of Dionysus (on whom see Karttunen 1989 pp. 212-19; Dahlquist 1996 pp. 270-6) at Nysa near a Mt. Meros (Megasth. *FGrH* 715 F4 §38.4; Arr. *Anab.* 5.2.6; Strab. 15.1.8 mentions the grapes from Mt. Meros). Although Mt. Meros cannot be identified with certainty, it is clear that it belongs in the northwest region, perhaps the Hindu Kush (see the study of Dahlquist op. cit. pp. 270-2). According to the *Arthashāstra* (2.25), wine originated in the northwest and in Chinese sources it seems that among the northwestern provinces the Nuristani, located on the southern slopes of the Hindu Kush, were especially known for their wine (Laufer 1919 p. 220; on the wine of the northwest and India see Karttunen op. cit. pp. 207-10).

five *orgyia*: 5 fathoms or *c.* 9 m.

three cubits: *c* 1.4 m.

three *orgyia*: 3 fathoms or *c.* 5.5 m.

In Indian it is called the *Ballade* which in Greek means 'useful': Cf. F45sα-β; According to Lassen (1874 vol. 2 p. 654), the spring's name comes from the Sanskrit term *baladā* meaning 'strength-giving'. Lindegger (1982 p. 75 n. 4), while acknowledging the possibility of this proposal, suggests that the name may also come from the Sanskrit term *bālyadā* meaning 'youth-giving'. The term is also used to describe a bullock and a medicinal plant, the *Physalis flexuosa* (see Monier-Williams s.v. 'balada'; see also McCrindle 1881 p. 304 n. 84). Lenfant (2004 p. 318 n. 883) following Fussman (1985) claims that these are fabricated terms and therefore Ctesias is not relating a genuine Indian name. The medicinal benefits of the spring indicate the Indians' discovery of the therapeutic aspects of mineral springs.

where the reed grows: Cf. §14.

there is a tribe of men numbering 30,000 ...: Cf. F45t, F52 where it is noted they are called the Pandarae (see note). The resume of Photius is a little confused as it seems to imply that the long-eared people known as the *Otoliknoi* (on whom see note below) are the same as the Pandarae, also known as the *Henotiktontes* ('those who give birth once'; cf. Megasth. *FGrH* 715 F27a-b) whereas Pliny and Tzetzes show that this is not the case. Clearly, Ctesias described two separate tribes which Photius hastily summarized into what seems to be one tribe. Ctesias' testimony is corroborated by Indian sources as well. The *Henotiktontes* are found in Sanskrit literature as *Ekagarbha* (Lassen 1874 vol. 2 p. 656 n. 1). The name Pandarae is connected to the term *pāndara* (OIA) meaning 'white' (Karttunen 1989 p. 207).

they have ears big enough to cover their arms: Cf. Megasth. *FGrH* 715 F27a-b who calls them Enotokoitai. In the *Mahābhārata* (2.28.44; 6.47.13) there is a race of long-eared people known as the *Karnaprāvarana* meaning 'the people who cover themselves with their ears' (André and Filliozat 1986 pp. 355-6 n. 121; Lassen 1874 vol. 2 p. 656 n. 1). The Indians often held the view that barbarous tribes had long ears. Thus the Indian sources mention other similar races such as the *Ushtrakarnās* ('camel-eared'), the *Oshthakarnās* (those who have ears close to their lips) and *Pānikarnās* (people who have hands for ears); see Wittkower 1942 p. 164. The *Rāmāyana* (4.40) mentions them along with the several other fabulous races like the One-Footed men (as Scylax also seems to do – cf. F51b). These long-eared people have been identified with Indian tribes from the hills who practised ear distension (Wheeler 1874 vol. 3 pp. 179-80 n. 42). On the tribes of long-eared people in literature see the study of Kirtley (1963).

he personally saw some of the things he wrote about while others he heard from first-hand witnesses: This line is parodied by Lucian (*VH* 1.2-4 = T11h). This passage clearly indicates that while Ctesias relates many accounts which can be found in Indian literature, he acquired all of his information by autopsy and from oral reports. Visitors from India likely told him of peoples and things taken from their great epics (see the Introduction, pp. 21-7, for a full discussion of Ctesias' sources).

F45a. the Indus River at its most narrow point is 40 stades across: Cf. F45 §1 and note.

F45bα. war elephants: Cf. F45 §7 and note, F1b §16 and note.
an Indian mahout: There is no reason to doubt that Aelian is directly following Ctesias here. The presence of an Indian mahout is further evidence that Ctesias encountered several Indians at the Persian court and obtained some of his information on India directly from the Indians themselves (see the Introduction, p. 23, for a full discussion). It is likely that the elephants Ctesias saw were gifts sent to the Persian king by the Indians; a century later Chandragupta, the founder of the Mauryan dynasty in India, gave 500 elephants to Seleucus Nicator as part of an agreement in exchange for territory (Strab. 15.2.9). The fact that they came with an Indian trainer shows that the Persians themselves had very little experience

in keeping elephants and that the beasts were probably a curiosity for them as well. In any case they certainly did not make much use of them in combat (see *Persika* F9 §7 on the use of elephants against Cyrus by the Indians who were fighting with the Derbikes; cf. Goukowski 1972 p. 475).

There are huge roosters: Cf. F45 §8; On the inclusion of this fragment into the corpus of Ctesias see Lenfant 2004 n. 891. This bird has been identified with the Impeyan monal, a pheasant (*Lophophorus impeyanus*) native to the Himalayas (Ball 1885 p. 305; see also Lassen 1874 p. 649 n. 1). The males (referred to as cocks) are adorned with beautifully bright shades of green, blue, turquoise, red and yellow. They also have a tall crest on the top of their heads (associated with the combs of roosters by Ctesias) which has often been compared to that of the peacock. Today, the variegated feathers of the bird are often sought after for ornamentation leading to a depletion of their stocks (*WOI* s.v. 'Birds' sect. 5).

F45c. the reeds of India: Cf. F45 §14 and note.

F45dα. the martichora: Cf. F45 §15 and note; F45dβ-δ.

F45dβ. In Indian it is called the martichora: The term is actually of Persian origin; cf. F45 §15 and note, F45dα, F45dγ, F45dδ.
it stretches its tail out flat like the Saka: The name denoted the peoples all along the northern fringes of Asia and those living north of the Black Sea. They were especially renowned

for their skill with the horse (F7b; Hdt. 9.71). The implication here is that the Saka while riding on horseback, were able to lay back flat with their head towards the tail of the horse and fire a bow over their heads at enemies behind them. Such a depiction of horsemanship is not implausible when one looks at the marvellous skill in equitation displayed today by the Cossacks who, it should be noted, live north of the Black Sea in an area once inhabited by the Saka.

F45dγ. the martichora: Cf. F45 §15 and note; F45dα, F45dβ, F45dδ.

F45dd. amongst these same men: i.e. the Ethiopians; Pliny misrepresents Ctesias and mistakenly places the martichora in Ethiopia. There was much confusion between Ethiopia and India for ancient commentators who often either saw no difference between the two or transposed features from one to the other (on this confusion see Arora 1982; Karttunen 1989 pp. 134-8). Although Ctesias seems to have been guilty of this to some degree, he certainly differentiated the two. In all the fragments of the *Indika*, he uses the term 'India' exclusively. He does mention 'Ethiopia' in the *Persika*, however it is always in clear reference to Africa. Immediately following a description of Semiramis' campaigns in Egypt, he discusses her conquest of Ethiopia (F1b §14-15), which is clearly a land in Africa wholly different from India (cf. F1b §22.4 where he calls them 'the Ethiopians near Egypt'). His description of a miraculous spring with water at the surface the colour of cinnabar is reminiscent of many of the springs discussed in the *Indika* showing that he viewed Ethiopia and India as similar, yet distinct places at the edge of the world.

the Mantichora: Although Pliny gives the form of the name which would become the standard in the Middle Ages into the present day (Manticore), the form given by Ctesias and reflected in the other parallel fragments more closely resembles the original Persian (see F45 §15 note for a full discussion; cf. also F45dα-γ).

F45eα. the so-called immortal flame: Cf. F45 §20 and note; F45eβ.

F45eβ. the flame is undying: Cf. F45 §20 and note; F45eα.

F45fα. those called the Pygmies: Cf. F45 §21 and note; F45fβ, F45fγ.
cotton garments: Cf. F45 §41 and note.
Throughout their childhood ...: Since this detail is omitted in the Photius excerpt, it is clear that the *Excerpta* of Constantine were likely made directly from the text of Ctesias rather than through the intermediary of Photius (Lenfant 2004 p. 323 n. 906).

F45fβ. the Pygmies: Cf. F45 §21 and note; F45fα, F45fγ.

F45fγ. The so-called Psylloi: Lenfant (2004) is perhaps right to include this passage in the fragments as the description of their minuscule livestock almost exactly corresponds to the account of the Pygmies' livestock in the other fragments (F45 §22; F45fα). However, it is unclear if Aelian is using Ctesias here directly (as he certainly does elsewhere – e.g. F45g) or an intermediary, and the use of the name Psylloi cannot easily be explained. Müller (1844 pp. 94-5) cites this passage as evidence that Ctesias used both names for this tribe, with the name Pygmies being the Greek term while the Psylloi represent the Indian name. However, the absence of the name Psylloi in two other parallel fragments clearly indicates that Ctesias never used the term. The Psylloi are frequently mentioned by other authors as inhabitants of Libya (e.g. Hecat. *FGrH* 1 F332; Hdt. 4.173; Strab. 2.5.33) but there is never any mention of their small stature or that of their livestock. In fact, the descriptions of the Libyan Psylloi bear no resemblance to the Pygmies. Thus, the contention of Bigwood (1989 pp. 309-10 n. 35) that Aelian simply confused the two is unsubstantiated since there is no sound reason for this simple confusion to occur. Moreover, Aelian explicitly says they are different from the Libyan tribe of the same name. It seems that a source after Ctesias (possibly Aelian himself) transferred the name of the Psylloi to that of the Indian Pygmies for reasons that remain unclear.

F45g. The Indians hunt hare and fox in the following way ...: Cf. F45 §24; The fact that Aelian says 'the Indians' rather than 'Pygmies' shows how Photius' careless summary of the *Indika* can lead to confusion as commentators have long credited the Pygmies with the use of falconry.

This is their method: The method of training the birds for falconry described here is strikingly accurate and is very similar to the techniques still employed in Turkestan at the beginning of the twentieth century (see the study of Lecoq 1914 pp. 5-6 for a description of the modern method of training; cf. also Karttunen 1981 p. 106). The precise and accurate description of these training techniques indicates that Ctesias likely obtained his information directly from a falconer, as this could hardly have been common knowledge. He may even have been able to witness a demonstration on their training techniques since a falconer could easily have brought his bird to the Persian court. Throughout the *Indika*, Ctesias is most accurate when describing things he was able to witness firsthand (cf. his description of the elephant [F1b §16.4; F45 §7; F45bα; F48a and b with notes] and of the parrot [F45 §8]) while the most fantastic elements of his narrative obviously stem from oral reports.

F45h. the griffin is an Indian animal: Cf. F45 §26 and note. **similar to what an artisan would draw:** see note on F45 §26; This statement has led some scholars to infer that Ctesias was actually describing an artistic rendition of a griffin perhaps from a Greek artifact (Karttunen 1989 pp. 178-9) or from Persian sculpture (Jacoby 1922 col. 2038). The variegated colours of this fantastic creature make such an assertion plausible (cf. note on F45 §45 for the possible influence of art on Ctesias' description of the unicorn).

F45iα. The sheep: Cf. F45 §27 and note; F45iβ; F45iγ. **these men:** i.e. the Indians.

a cubit wide: *c.* 46 cm.

F45iβ. the Indians have sheep ...: Cf. F45 §27 and note;
F45iα; F45iγ.
a cubit in width: *c.* 46 cm.
ten *minae* of fat ... only five: *c.* 4.3 kg and 2.2 kg respectively.
They make oil: The Indians were very fond of cooking with
oil, usually using sesame oil or mustard oil (Auboyer 1965 p.
196). See note on F45 p. 112.
three *minae* ... up to four: *c.* 1.3-1.7 kg.

F45iγ. I hear that the goats and ewes ...: Cf. F45 §27 and
note; F45iα; F45iβ. On the inclusion of this passage into the
Fragments see Lenfant 2004 p. 325 n. 919.

F45kα. there are no swine in India: Cf. F45 §27 and note;
F45kβ; F45kγ; F45kδ; F45kε.

**F45kβ. Ctesias says there are neither wild nor tame pigs
in India:** Cf. F45 §27 and note; F45kα; F45kγ; F45kδ; F45kε.

F45kγ. there are no swine in India either tame or wild: Cf.
F45 §27 and note; F45kα; F45kβ; F45kδ; F45kε.
No Indian would ever eat the meat of swine: While in
certain parts of India the pig is despised, it is consumed by
some Hindus (Ball 1885 p. 286 and note on F45 §27).
anymore than he would that of a human: Cf. F45kδ and
note.

F45kδ. They say that there are no swine in India: Lenfant (2004) rightly includes this passage in the corpus of the fragments based on its similarity to F45kγ.

they would never eat human flesh: In fact there is ample evidence of cannibals living in the northwest region of the country. According to Herodotus, an Indian tribe known as the Kallatiae (3.38) and another called the Padaioi (3.99) are known to eat the bodies of their parents. Pliny (*NH* 6.20.55) mentions a cannibalistic tribe called the *Casiri* (cf. also Megasth. *FGrH* 715 F27b who mentions a tribe of cannibals but offers no name for them). Cannibals were also known to Indian literature such as the *Nāgas* (*NīlP* 68-73) and the *Pishācas* (*Rājat* 1.184; *NīlP* 203-4), inhabitants of the Kashmir region, and the *Rākshasas* (see Karttunen 1989 pp. 197-202 for a full discussion).

F45kε. this king: Arganthonius of Gades.
the same assertion is made about the Indians by Ctesias: Cf. F45 §32 and note.

F45l. the snake: Cf. F45 §33 and note.

F45m. The Indians call it *Dikairon* ... *Dikaion*: Cf. F45 §34 and note.
This death would bring freedom from pain: This description of the effects of the Dikairon's dung as freedom from pain bears a striking resemblance to the drug *nepenthe* described in the Odyssey (4.218-32); cf. Becerra Romero 2007 pp. 257-8.

the king himself and his mother: Artaxerxes II and Parysatis.

F45nα. the *parebon*: Cf. F45 §35 and note; F45nβ.

F45nβ. *parebon*: Cf. F45 §35 and note; F45α.

F45o. the Hypobarus: On the name and identification of this river see note on F45 §36; cf. F45oβ.
the *psittachora*: On the name and identification of this tree see note on F45 §36; cf. F45oβ.

F45oβ. the *spabaros*: The preferred form of the name and the one most likely given by Ctesias (see note on F45 §36; cf. F45oα).
the *zetachora*: Cf. F45 §36 and note; F45oα.
the Pontic nut: the hazelnut.
who have the head of a dog ...: Cf. F45 §37 and note; F45 §40-3; F45pα-γ.
They eat ... the raw meat from wild animals which they hunt: Actually, Ctesias says that the Cynocephaloi cook the meat from their game in the sun (F45 §40). Psellos has perhaps misunderstood the process of making a jerky out of meat and because of the absence of fire cooking viewed the product as 'raw' (see also Lenfant 2004 p. 326 n. 932 who rejects the idea of Maas 1924 that Psellos misread the text).

F45pα. a race of men with the head of a dog: Cf. F45 §37 and note; F45 §40-3; F45pβ-γ.
They are armed for the hunt with talons ...: Although

Ctesias mentions the talons of the Cynocephaloi (F45 §37), nowhere else in the fragments does it say they were used for hunting. In fact, Ctesias explicitly says that they hunted with bows and javelins (F45 §42). Furthermore, nowhere else in the fragments is it indicated that they specifically feasted on birds, but rather that they ate wild game (F45 §40, 42; F45oβ; F45pγ). This indicates that Pliny is likely using another source for this information, probably Megasthenes who in turn drew much of his information on the Cynocephaloi from Ctesias. He likely did refer directly to Ctesias for their longevity, as Megasthenes makes no mention of it. As such, this passage may provide valuable insight into the account of Megasthenes. He evidently misinterpreted (or embellished) the description of their talons as being used for hunting while omitting the detail about their longevity.

F45pβ. amber-producing trees: Cf. F45 §36 and note.
dog-headed peoples: Cf. F45 §37, §40-3 and notes; F45oβ; F45pα; F45pγ.

F45pγ. There are creatures in India the size of dung beetles: Cf. F45 §39 and note.
the amber-producing trees: Cf. F45 §36 and note.
the revered Sardian robes: Sardian purple was highly prized among the Greeks (Ar. *Pax* 1173-4).
Cynocephaloi: Cf. F45 §37, §40-3 and notes; F45oβ; F45pα-β.

F45q. there are wild asses in India: Cf. F45 §45 and note.
They say their astragaloi are black ...: Actually, Ctesias says

that the astragaloi of the unicorn are red like cinnabar. Either Aelian is basing his description on dark colored gaming dice made from astragaloi, or he is following a source other than Ctesias for this information. The phrase 'they say' seems to indicate the latter and that Aelian chose to follow a later source which contradicted Ctesias on the colour of the astragalos (see note on F45 §45).

F45r. the worm: Cf. F45 §46 and note.
a ten-year-old boy would hardly be able to embrace it: Ctesias is fond of describing the width of objects in terms of a human's embrace (cf. his description of the Indian reed F45 §14).
a *pygon* in length: *c*. 39 cm.
ten *kotylae*: *c*. 2.7 litres.
he takes the cities by burning them to ashes: This account describes a substance similar to Greek fire which was invented in late antiquity by Alexandrian chemists. It is possible that such tales of besieging cities with unquenchable fire inspired the Byzantine chemists to search for a formula for creating so powerful a substance.
a *kotyla*: 0.27 litre.

F45sα. one of the lakes in India: Cf. F45 §49 and note; F45sβ.
On another lake oil floats: Cf. F45 §25.
the so-called white disease: A type of leprosy (Hdt. 1.138; Hp. *Prorrh*. 2.43; Arist. *HA* 518a13).

F45sβ. There is a spring in India: Cf. F45 §49; F45sα.

F45t. Amongst a certain Indian race: Cf. F45 §50 and note.

F46a. the so-called Cynamolgoi: Cf. F46b; Some scholars have concluded that the Cynamolgoi were not treated by Ctesias but rather by Agatharcides of Cnidus (§60) who locates them in Ethiopia (Lassen 1982 p. 67; Karttunen 1984 p. 35). To be sure, there was great confusion surrounding these people for the ancient writers. Pollux (F46b) claims that the Cynamolgoi were dogs and Pliny (*NH* 6.195), who places them in Ethiopia, says they had dog-heads (*Cynamolgi caninis capitibus*). However, Aelian, who here gives the most detailed account of the Cynamolgoi, clearly shows them to be human and offers no indication that they had dog-heads thus indicating that they were a tribe wholly independent of the Cynocephaloi. It is doubtful that Aelian confused the Cynamolgoi with the Cynocephaloi and errantly attributed the former to Ctesias rather than his countryman Agatharchides. This hypothesis rests on the unlikely assumption that both Aelian and Pollux are guilty of the same mistake independently since they both name Ctesias as their source (as already noted by Lenfant 2004 pp. 327-8 n. 950; it is clear that both Aelian and Pollux read Ctesias directly since Aelian cites him numerous times in his work and Pollux names Ctesias as a source on one other occasion [F1pγ]). Indeed Pollux displays carelessness since he erroneously claims that the Cynamolgoi were dogs rather than breeders of them. However, it is more difficult to accuse Aelian of such negligence to detail since often his citations of Ctesias conform accurately with other parallel fragments (e.g. F45dβ and F45 §15). There is no valid reason to believe that Ctesias did not give an account of both the Cynocephaloi and the Cynamolgoi. Agatharchides was probably familiar with Ctesias' Cynamolgoi (Fraser II p. 789 n. 246) and his transference of them to Ethiopia is simply a return to the old confusion between Africa and India by the ancients. Furthermore, there is some evidence that the Cynamolgoi may be of Indian origin. In the *Amarakosa* (2.10.44-6), the sixth-century Sanskrit lexicon, there is mention of a tribe of outcasts called the *shvapāka*, whose name means 'dog-cookers' (White 1991 pp. 71-2). The confusion between the two may have originated with Ctesias himself if one accepts the proposal of Marquart (1913 pp. ccviii-ccix) that the tribal name he gives to the Cynocephaloi, the Kalystrioi, is related to the OP **sa-dauxštr* from the Sanskrit *shva-duhitr* 'milker of dogs' (but see note on F45 §37 for problems with this suggestion). Ultimately, it seems that Ctesias described both Cynamolgoi and Cynocephaloi as two independent tribes of India, perhaps in consecutive passages, thus leading to the confusion for later authors.

F46b. The Cynamolgoi are dogs: Obviously a mistake either by Pollux or by a copyist since the testimony of Aelian (F46a) shows clearly that the Cynamolgoi were a tribe of men who reared dogs (see F46a and note).

take their nourishment from the milk of cows: Pollux seems to be conflating two separate accounts of the Cynamolgoi, one of which omits the practice of drinking dog's milk (thus nullifying the meaning of their name) and instead claiming that they get their nourishment from cows rather than dogs (cf. Diod. 3.31 who seems to be loosely following Agatharchides).

F47a. the Indian spring called the Sila: On the name Sila cf. F47b and note; The Sila has the exact opposite features of the *Ballade* (F45 §49; cf. Andre and Filiozat 1986 pp. 429-30 n. 558). The spring is first mentioned in Greek literature by Hellanicus (*FGrH* 4 F190) and later by Megasthenes (*FGrH* 715 F10b), Democritus and Aristotle (apud Strabo 15.1.38), and Diodorus (2.37 who seems to be following Megasthenes). Herodotus (3.23) describes a river with similar qualities in Ethiopia. The Sila appears in several Indian and Chinese sources thus showing that the story has an Eastern origin (Lassen 1874 vol. 2 pp. 657-8). In all the Eastern accounts, the Sila is actually a river rather than a spring (although Megasthenes mentions a river beginning from a spring). In the *Mahābhārata* (2.48.2-4) and the *Rāmāyana* (4.42.37-8), the boundary of the paradise Uttarakuru is formed by the river *Shilā* ('stone') or *Shailodā* ('stone-water') which can only be crossed by boats made of the *kīcaka* reed (on which see F45 §14 and note) because all other objects turn to stone upon coming into contact with the water. Chinese sources refer to the river as *Jo-shui* meaning 'soft-water' in which not even a feather can float (Lindegger 1982 pp. 75-81 for a full discussion of these sources). In Buddhist literature it is called the *Sīdā* ('sink'; see note below) because everything in it sinks. See also the studies of Karttunen 1985 and 1989 pp. 186-9; Sachse 1982.

F47b. called the Side: This has long been thought to be a corruption of the name Sila, which is the form appearing in several other sources both Greek and Eastern (see note above). Based on the similarity of the Greek lambda to the delta, Mayhoff proposed to correct the text to read Sile (arguing that Pliny misread or had a copy of Ctesias with the erroneous transcription of ΣΙΔΩΝ instead of ΣΙΛΩΝ). While this emendation is generally accepted, the form Side can be corroborated in Buddhist literature. In the *Nimijātaka* (*J* 541 vv. 424-5), the river is called the *Sīdā*. However, the prevalence of the form Sila in the Greek sources, especially authors such as Megasthenes who most certainly followed Ctesias, coupled with the fact the form Sila appears elsewhere in the fragments of Ctesias (F47a) indicate that the Cnidian most likely gave the form Sila. The fact the form Side also appears in Buddhist literature is merely coincidental (see Karttunen 1985).

F48a. what Ctesias writes about the sperm of elephants: Cf. F48b and note.

F48b. what he says about the sperm of elephants: Ctesias evidently gave a detailed discourse on the elephant but surprisingly little of it survives. Unfortunately, Photius quickly glosses over this account no doubt because of its mundane nature (F45 §7). Apart from this obviously false statement regarding their sperm, much of what can be extracted from Ctesias account of elephants has been shown to be accurate (see notes on F45 §7 and F1b §16.4).

The statement of Aristotle comes amidst a discussion of the general qualities of sperm in which he also criticizes Herodotus for claiming that the sperm of Ethiopians is black.

F49a. Ctesias of Cnidus: Arrian spells his name Κτησίης in an apparent attempt at Ionization since his *Indika* was written in Ionic. In his *Anabasis*, he uses the normal spelling (T11g; Lenfant 2004 p. 11 n. 39).
the territory of India is equal to the size of the rest of Asia: Cf. F49b; This statement corresponds well with Cteisas' overall view of India as an enormous land with an enormous population (cf. F45 §2).

F49b. India is no smaller than the rest of Asia: Cf. F49a.

F50. it is not permissible for the king to get drunk: Cf. Megasth. *FGrH* 715 F32 §55 who also mentions a prohibition on intoxication for the king. While the Indians were familiar with wine and often fermented alcoholic beverages from other fruits (cf. note on F45 §48), drinking was strictly condemned by the Brahmans.

F51a. the same race: This is a continuation of F45t.
the Monocoli ... also called the Sciapodes: Cf. F51b; F60; Pliny seems to have erroneously described the Monocoli and the Sciapodes as one tribe, a mistake which influenced medieval depictions of the Sciapodes. Scylax, the first Greek author to write on the Sciapodes (cf. F51b and note) describes

them as having two very large feet (note the use of the plural) and elsewhere (F60) it is shown that Ctesias too depicted them with two feet (Lenfant 2004 pp. 329-30 n. 966; see also Karttunen 1989 p. 132 n. 74 who accepts the one-footedness of the Sciapodes). This is confirmed by Indian sources who often make mention of one-footed people and Sciapodes, always independent of each other, but describe them as demons. The Monocoli are found in the *Harivamsha* (Vul. 9553), which came after Ctesias but contained more ancient traditions, where they are called the *Ekapāda* ('Those with one foot'). In the same list there is also mention of the *Tālajangha* ('Those with a palm for a leg' – see Filliozat 1981 pp. 103-5). Likewise, both tribes appear in a list of monstrosities in Buddhist literature. In the *Lalitavistara* (XXI) there is mention of both *Ekapādaka* ('those who have one foot'; they also appear in both the Rāmāyana and the Mahābhārata – cf. Lassen 1874 vol. 2 pp. 656-7 n. 1) and *Karotapāda* ('those who have a branch for a foot'). See Andre and Filiozat 1986 p. 355 n. 121.

those who lack necks and have eyes on their shoulders: Cf. Hdt. 4.191 who places this tribe in Libya. Elsewhere (5.8.46) Pliny describes the Blemmyes who are an African tribe of men who have no heads but eyes and a mouth on their chest.

There are also satyrs in the mountains ...: It is generally believed that this passage is not attributed to Ctesias (although Jacoby, acknowledging that it is not from Ctesias, nevertheless includes it). The satyrs of India have been identified with monkeys, most notably langurs (Andre and Filiozat 1986 pp. 355-6 n. 121; see Puskás and Kádár 1980 on the Indian satyrs).

Fig. 2. *Monsters of India and Africa.* Woodcut from Sebastian Munster, *Cosmographiae Universalis*, Basil 1550, reproduced by permission of the Rare Book and Manuscript Library of the University of Illinois at Urbana-Champaign.

F51b. Scylax of Caryanda: Although most people accept that this refers to the Scylax who was commissioned by Darius to explore the Indus (Hdt. 4.44), Herrmann (1929 col. 518) instead proposes that this refers to the *Periplous* of Pseudo-Scylax (*c.* 350 BCE). This would make Ctesias the oldest source for these fantastic tribes. Unfortunately, there is not enough evidence to corroborate such a claim, but Tzetzes seems to take Scylax as the ultimate source for these peoples.

the Sciapodes: Cf. F51a and note; F60.

The Otoliknoi: Cf. F45 §50 and note.

the Monophthalmoi: Cf. Megasth. *FGrH* 715 F27a-b.

the Henotiktontes: Cf. F45 §50 and note; Megasth. *FGrH* 715 F27a-b.

F52. the Pandarae: Cf. F45 §50 and note; F45t.

who live for 200 years: Ctesias says the same about several tribes of Indians; see note on F45 §32.

Other Works

On the Tributes of Asia

F53. *On the Tributes of Asia*: On this work see the Introduction, pp. 34-6.

he never mentions pepper or vinegar: Polyaenus (Strat. 4.3.32) catalogues the ingredients for the king's lunch and dinner. He claims that he obtained his information from a bronze pillar, an assertion most feel is fabricated. In fact, it is very likely that his source is Ctesias himself. His account, which also omits pepper, only includes vinegar among the commodities distributed by the king, but not among those consumed by him (cf. the study of Lewis 1987; Briant 2002 pp. 286-92; see also the more recent study of Amigues 2003). On the king's meals see also Heracleides *FGrH* 689 F2; Deinon *FGrH* 690 F4, F12, F24. See also F63 and note.

F54. the Tapyroi: Cf. F1b §2.3 and note.

Periodos (Periegesis, Periploi)

Book I

F55. *Periploi*: On this work see the Introduction, pp. 34-6.

F56. the Tibarenoi in the territory of the Mossynoikoi:

These tribes are located in the southeastern region of the Black Sea; cf. Hdt. 3.94, 7.78.

Book II

F57. Ctesias claims in Book II: Although the title of the work is not mentioned, it seems that this refers to the *Periodos* (although Müller 1844 p. 106 attributes it to *On Mountains*). It is clear from the other fragments that Ctesias dealt extensively with the regions of the Black Sea in this work. However, it is possible that this citation comes from a passing reference to these mountains in Ctesias' description of Ninus' Armenian campaign which was discussed early in the *Persika* (F1b §1.8-19).

F58. Tiriza: Otherwise unknown. There is a cape on the coast of the Black Sea called variably Tiriza (*Anonym. peripl.* p. E 75), Tirizis (Strab. 7.319), and Tiristis (Ptolem. 3.10.3). The site, always referred to as a cape (ἄκρα), is located in lower Moesia (Scythia) on the west coast of the Black Sea in modern Bulgaria. It later took the name Γαλιάκρα in Byzantine sources (now called Caliacra). Ctesias may have been misinformed as to its location on the Black Sea and mistakenly placed it on the southern coast in Paphlagonia. The name of the site is Thracian (*ter*, *tir* meaning 'end' or 'point') thus confirming its true location on the western coast of the Black Sea (Fluss 1937 col. 1446-7).

Ctesias calls them Tiribizanoi in Book II: cf. note above on the omission of the title of the work.

Book unknown

F60. Sciapodes: Cf. F51a-b and note.

Periplous of Asia: Harpocration is the only author to mention this title. Elsewhere the work is simply called the *Periplous* (F55), the *Periodos* (F56), and the *Periegesis* (F59). It seems evident that these are all variant titles of the same work. The mention of the Sciapodes in this work is difficult to explain. Ctesias mentions them in the *Indika* (F51a-b) where he clearly locates them in India (from F45t), and an analysis of Indian sources shows that they are clearly of Indian origin (see note on F51a). Ctesias may have mentioned them in both works, in which case he would have located them on the eastern edge of Asia. However, in the *Indika* Ctesias locates them further east of the men with no necks indicating that they, like other fabulous races, are on the fringes of the world, not the fringes of Asia. If in fact he did mention them in the *Periplous*, it was likely a passing reference rather than a full discussion as occurred in the *Indika*. Ultimately, Lenfant (2004 p. 331 n. 978) may be right to want to attribute this fragment to the *Indika* rather than the *Periplous*. Although there are only a few fragments from the latter work, there is no indication of any other fabulous tribes discussed (see the Introduction, pp. 34-6, for full discussion) giving more plausibility to Lenfant's suggestion.

Fragments of unknown works

F61a. in his history: Cf. F61b; This fragment may come from the *Periplous* (F57 and note). However, it may equally have originated from the *Persika* in the account of Ninus' expedition in Armenia (cf. F1b §1.8-19), or perhaps the banishment of the eunuch Artoxares (F14 §43, F15 §50).

F61b. in Armenia ...: Cf. F61a and note.

F62. Book III of Ctesias: This fragment is too scanty to decipher which work this belongs to. It may be either the *Periodos* or the *Persika* both of which had at least three books.

F63. The origin of pepper: This passage is most likely not from Ctesias. Elsewhere we see that Ctesias conspicuously omitted pepper in his discussion of the king's dinner (F53) and there is no reason to believe he did so in this passage, which likely stems from a later source (see Hansen 1965). Pepper comes from the dried berry of the *Piper negrum*, which is a vine (as Maximus asserts) indigenous to Southern India. It may have originated in the Western Ghats on the western peninsula of the Indian subcontinent. The word originates from the Sanskrit *pippalī* (Steier 1938 col. 1421-5 for a full discussion). The earliest account of pepper in Greek sources is found in Hippocrates (*Morb. Mulier* 1.81 [8 p. 202 L]) who refers to it as an Indian drug (φάρμακον).

F64. The island of Thule: It is difficult to determine in which work Ctesias would have discussed the island of Thule which belongs to the northern edge of the world. Nowhere else in the fragments is there any indication of an interest in the north. On this island cf. Strab. 1.4.2-3; 2.5.8; Plin. *NH* 4.104; Stat. *Silv*. 5.1.91; Sil. Ital. 597; Iuven. 15.112. For a full discussion

see De Anna 1998; MacDonald 1936 col. 627-30; Romm 1992
pp. 158-62, 206-11.
when the sun is in Cancer: 21 June to 22 July.

F65. Heridanus: There is little agreement among ancient
commentators for the Eridanos, as this passage indicates.
Hesiod (*Th*. 338) makes the earliest mention of the Eridanos as
the child of Ocean and Tethys. Since Ctesias locates the river
in India, it is tempting to attribute this fragment to the *Indika*.

F66. the Erythran Sea: the Red Sea.

Medical treatises

F67. The first was Ctesias of Cnidus: Ctesias' criticism
of Hippocrates here began what would be a long-running
debate over the proper method for setting a dislocated hip
(Jouanna 1999 p. 435 n. 14). Because Ctesias was only a
generation after Hippocrates, this passage has been taken
as support for identifying the treatise *On Joints* as a
genuine Hippocratic work (see however Jouanna op. cit.
p. 65 for the difficulties encountered when trying to
identify authentic works of Hippocrates). The criticisms
of Ctesias have also been taken as a reflection of the
rivalry between the Cnidian and Coan schools of medicine.
This rivalry, long the source of dispute amongst modern
scholars (Lonie 1978), was neither violent nor hateful.
None of the malicious stories of Hippocrates committing
plagiarism and arson stem from his Cnidian rivals (the

earliest report of such slanderous tales comes from Andreas, the third-century BCE physician to the Egyptian king Ptolemy IV Philopator, apud Polyb. 5.81.6; cf. Plin. *NH* 29.1-2 for the account, based on Varro, of his burning of the temple of Asclepius after consulting inscriptions to hide his sources; see also Tzetz. 963-5). As can be seen from Ctesias' criticism, the rivalry was strictly professional (Gal. *De methodo medendi* 1.1.6). There was even an association (κοίνον) formed between Asclepiads from the two schools, as is shown by an inscription found at Delphi (Rougemont 1977 vol. 1 122-4 no. 12; see also note below).

his relative (for this man too was a member of the Asclepiads): The Asclepiads were two branches of the same family that claimed descent from Asclepius. Although the term later came to describe all physicians, in its proper and more narrow sense it only refers to members of this family, regardless of their profession (Tzetz. 10.721-7). Thus when Galen refers to Ctesias as a relative of Hippocrates, he means it in the strictest sense of the term. The Asclepiads passed their knowledge down from father to son (F68 and note) beginning with Asclepius himself and his two sons Podalirius and Machaon (Hom. *Il.* 2.729-32). An inscription from Delphi indicates that the Asclepiad lineage was only transmitted by male descent. This inscription is also significant in showing the association between the two branches of Asclepiads (see note above) and the special privilege they enjoyed at Delphi (Rougemont 1977 vol. I pp. 122-4 no. 12). On the Asclepiads see especially the study of Jouanna 1999 pp. 10-12, 50-2.

F68. The treatise of Ctesias on hellebore: On these medical treatises see the Introduction, pp. 34-6.

In my father's time and my grandfather's time: This passage clearly reveals that the medicinal knowledge of the Asclepiads was familial and passed down from father to son (F67 and note). It also shows that Ctesias was a true Asclepiad and not just a physician who received the title based on his profession.

hellebore: Black hellebore (*Helleborus cyclophyllus*) was a small plant used as a purgative by the ancients to remedy illness (see for ex. Hipp. *Coan Prognoses* 2.304 [V. 650L]), but the term hellebore can also refer to white hellebore (*veratrum album*; cf. Plin. *NH* 25.48). It was also called *melampodion* (e.g. Theophr. 9.10.4) and *polyrrhizon*. It was often used as a cure for madness and paralysis (Plin. *NH* 25.54) along with several other diseases including leprosies and toothaches. When inserted as a suppository it can be used to induce an abortion (Hp. *Mul.* 8.154; Dsc. 4.162.1-3; Riddle 1992 pp. 54-5; see also Kapparis 2002 pp. 13-16 for a discussion of the use of herbs to induce abortion). Ctesias' statement regarding the safety of the drug by his time is confirmed by Pliny (*NH* 25.51) who states that in his day some academics took it to sharpen their minds (see also *NH* 25.59-61 on how to use hellebore). See Theophr. *HP* 9.9.2; 9.14.4). On hellebore see the studies of André 1954 and Girard 1988.

Fragments of doubtful authenticity

F69. Ctesias, Herodotus, Diodorus ...: Nowhere else in the fragments does Ctesias mention a Sesostris and at no point is there any indication he may have. Sesostris is always mentioned as king of Egypt rather than the Assyrians. The accounts of Herodotus (2.102-10) and Diodorus (1.53-7 who calls him Sesoosis) afford no place for this anecdote as there is no indication that Sesostris mistreated any of the kings he conquered (Diod. 1.55.10 even says he acted mildly towards all conquered peoples). At the conclusion of his summary Diodorus (1.56.5) compares the conquests of Sesostris with those of Semiramis described by Ctesias (given by Diodorus himself at 2.14). The naming of Ctesias here was likely the cause of confusion for Tzetzes thus resulting in his inclusion of Ctesias among the authors who treat Sesostris. The anecdote likely comes from Theophylactus Simocatta (6.11.8-17).

F70. Xenophon wrote a history of Cyrus: In the *Cyropaidea* (8.3.49), Xenophon speaks of gratitude and repayment of favors and (8.7.3) giving thanks for favour received from the gods, but never makes any mention of chastisement for ingratitude.

Ctesias and Herodotus wrote about the Persian custom: There is nothing in Herodotus about this custom nor is there any reason to believe Ctesias wrote about it. As he has done elsewhere (F69; F71), Tzetzes has carelessly listed a series of authors on Persian history without verifying his statements.

F71. Herodotus, Diodorus, Ctesias ...: Cf. F69 on Tzetzes' habit of grouping these authors together. It seems clear he misread Ctesias who certainly would have made such comments regarding India rather than Arabia in comparison to India. Throughout the *Indika*, Ctesias makes constant reference to the Indians as a just and blessed people.

F72. The historiographer says: It is difficult to decipher if the historian in question is Ctesias. To be sure, Arsames appears in the *Persika* as satrap of Egypt (F14 §38; the text gives the name Sarsamas but this is likely a corruption; see note ad loc. See also F15 §49 where he is called Arxanes) and Ctesias describes an Indian tribe whose children have beautiful teeth (F45 §50). If this is an authentic fragment then it likely comes from the *Persika* and is a reference to the satrap of Egypt.

False fragments

On Mountains

F73. the *antipathes*: Dioscorides (5.122) takes this stone for black coral and says that, like regular coral, it is used to reduce excrescences and cicatrize wounds among other remedies. He says nothing of its use to treat dull-white leprosy or leprosy. This term does not appear in any of the Hippocratic writings and is not employed until Hellenistic times leading many to doubt this fragment's authenticity. Although Ctesias makes several mentions of leprosy (F14 §43) including treatments for it (F45 §49), the fact that this work is not mentioned anywhere else is cause for doubt.

Mt. Teuthras: A mountain in Mysia in northwest Asia Minor named for the mythical king who took in Auge, the daughter of Aleus and raised her son Telephus (Apollod. 2.7.4; Paus. 8.4).

On Rivers

F74. Alpheus: A river in the Peloponnese.

Book I of his treatise *On Rivers*: The medicinal aspect of this fragment renders it plausible that this is a genuine work of Ctesias. However, as with the treatise *On Mountains*, the fact that it is nowhere else mentioned invites suspicion (F73 and note).

Interpolations

F75. *The tales of Ctesias of Cnidus*: The passages of F75 and F76 appear in only two manuscripts and their authenticity is highly suspect (see Diller 1969; on the inclusion of these last two fragments with the corpus of Ctesias see Lenfant 2004 pp. 334-5 n. 1001). One is the Codex Monacensis Graecus 287, a fifteenth-century manuscript containing astrological excerpts, religious and ethnographic writings, and an abridgment of the *Indika* that follows Photius but incorporates some new data. The other is the Codex Oxoniensis, Holkham Graecus 110, which contains similar material (see Solomou 2007 pp. 13-16 for full descriptions). To be sure, certain elements in these texts, such as the material on the Seres, seem to date to a time period later than Ctesias (see note below; Janvier 1984 p. 264). However, the passages certainly conform to Ctesias' style and follow many of the same motifs and literary constructions found elsewhere in the *Indika*, often with striking resemblance. The unusual size and longevity of the Seres recalls several tribes of the *Indika* (e.g. the Pygmies [F45 §21] are exceedingly small while the Pandarae [F52

§28], the Indians [F45 §32] and the Cynocephaloi [F45 §43], like the Seres, can live as long as 200 years). Like other hybrids in the *Indika*, the krokottas displays human characteristics (cf. the martichora [F45 §15]; the parrot [F45 §8]), and the author describes specific attributes of the animal by comparing them to creatures well known in the Greek world (e.g. the parrot is depicted as the size of a falcon [F45 §8]; the martichora the size of a lion [F45 §15]; the griffin the size of a wolf [F45 §26], etc.). The flocks in Calchis that lack bile and have flesh so bitter that it renders them inedible are strongly reminiscent of Ctesias' unicorn (F45 §45), which, unlike other solid-hoofed animals, has bile in the liver and flesh too bitter to eat. Finally, there are descriptions of miraculous springs, a favourite topic for Ctesias. That these passages do not deal with India cannot be taken as evidence that they are spurious since elsewhere Ctesias discusses matters as far west as Zacynthus, Naxos and Sicily (F45 §20). While it is uncertain whether Ctesias ever discussed these topics, at least it should be accepted that the excerpts of F75 and F76 are not fabrications on the part of the excerptor and can be traced to other sources (as even Diller admits).

The Seres: Aside from this passage, the earliest reference to the Seres is by Apollodorus of Artemita (apud Strab. 11.11.1) who says that they were annexed along with the Phrynoi by the Bactrian Greeks. The Seres were a tribe dwelling on the fringes of the Greek world from whom silk was obtained, often equated with the Chinese. However, the people mentioned both here and by Apollodorus are more likely middlemen who traded along the Silk Road (Karttunen 1997a p. 285, 338). They became popular subjects for writers of the Roman period (e.g. Plin. *NH* 6.20; Hor. *Car.* 3.19.25-8; et al.). On the Seres and the various attempts at their identification see the studies of Herrmann 1923, Janvier 1984 and Sergent 1998; see also Schwartz 1986 and Solomou 2007 pp. 198-9.

thirteen cubits: *c.* 6 m.

they live for more than 200 years: The Seres' longevity is attested elsewhere, although with little agreement on how long they lived. Strabo (15.1.34, 37) claims they lived more than 130 years while Lucian (*Macr.* 5) says they live as long as 300 years.

the Gaïtros River: Perhaps the Ganges. Since the name Gaïtros appears nowhere else, this is likely a scribal error, possibly for ΓΑΓΓΟΥ (first proposed by Müller 1884 p. 87, accepted by Solomou 2007 p. 199).

there are savage men: This tribe, called *theriodeis* ('savage'), is also mentioned by Ptolemy (7.2.21; at 7.3.1 he seems to use the term Theriodeis as the name of the tribe rather than an adjective). Julius Honorius refers to both the Seres and Theriodeis in the same order but curiously describes them as towns rather than tribes (*Seres oppidum, Theriodes oppidum: Excerpta* 6 in Riese 1878). He also mentions a river named Theriodes that flows into the Caspian Sea (*Excerpta* 7).

F76. For this passage see note on F75.

In Ethiopia: Cf. F45dδ on the confusion between Ethiopia and India. On the problems with this reference to Ethiopia see note on F75.

there is a creature called the krokottas: Often identified with the spotted hyena (*Crocuta crocuta*), which is native to Africa (e.g. Ball 1881 p. 281; Karttunen 1997 p. 175; McCrindle 1881 p. 305 n. 86 refers to it simply as 'a sort of hyena'). The Greeks had been aware of the hyena at least since the time of Herodotus (4.192). Herodotus' ὕαινα certainly refers to the striped hyena (*Hyena hyena*; cf. Arist. *HA* 579b15, 594a31) which is widely distributed between India, Africa, Arabia and Asia Minor, being the only species of hyena found outside of Africa (on the *Hyaenidae*, see Funk forthcoming a; I am grateful to Dr Funk for kindly supplying me with advanced copies of his work). While there is a consensus among modern scholars that the Greeks differentiated between two types of hyena (using the terms ὕαινα to describe the striped hyena and krokottas for the spotted hyena, see Steier 1924 col. 762), the identification of the fantastic krokottas remains uncertain. The ancient sources are far from unanimous in their descriptions of this fabulous beast. Agatharchides (*GGM* 77 = Phot. cod. 250 c.39) and Diodorus (3.35.10) both state it is a composite of a wolf and a dog. Pliny describes the *crocotta* as a cross between a wolf and a dog (*NH* 8.30), although he also mentions the *corocotta* (a hybrid of a hyena and a lion; ib. 8.45), as well as the similarly named *leucrocotta* (which shares several attributes with the *corocotta*; ib. 8.30), apparently seeing all three as distinct animals. Aelian (7.22) was the first to compare the hyena to the krokottas, which he calls the *korokotta*; however he offers no physical description, only focusing on the creatures' fantastic vocal capabilities. Similarly problematic is the identification of the horizontally striped animal labelled krokottas in the Palestrina Nile Mosaic – presumably the only pictorial evidence for this creature to have survived from antiquity (Funk forthcoming b). There is a drawing of a spotted hyena labelled as krokottas on the Artemidorus Papyrus, however there is much speculation concerning its authenticity (see the convincing arguments for forgery by Janko 2009) and it will not be discussed here.

The krokottas' 'bone-crushing' jaws are fitting for either the striped or the spotted hyena, and its most striking feature, the ability to mimic human voices – often attributed to the 'laughing' calls of the spotted hyena – can be compared to sounds of other animals, such as the howls of the jackal (*Canis aureus*). Consequently, association of the krokottas with the spotted hyena cannot rest solely on its physical description. Arguments for this identification based on the location of the animal in Africa are similarly inconclusive. Like Ctesias, all the earliest sources, including Agatharchides, Diodorus and Dalion (*FGrH* 666 F1), place the krokottas in Ethiopia. In this case the difficulty lies in the linguistics of the name, since no known African term bears any phonemic resemblance to krokottas (see Funk forthcoming b). In fact, the term has been plausibly linked to the Sanskrit word for jackal (*kroshtuka*; Prakrit: *kotthāraka;* Schwanbeck 1846 p. 3 and Lassen 1874 vol. 2 p. 650), confirming the evidence of late sources such as Dio Cassius (77.1.3-4) and Porphyry (*Abst.* 3.4) that locate the animal in India (see also *Peripl. M. Rubr.* 50). Arguments against the identification with the jackal include this animal's relatively innocuous behavior and the lack of powerful jaws.

Ultimately, the true nature of the krokottas remains elusive.

In Euboea in the land of Calchis the flocks of that region: Cf. Arist. *PA* 676b35-677a5. On the similarities of these sheep to the unicorn see note on F75.

the Maurousian Gates: Possibly the Pillars of Heracles (i.e. the Straits of Gibraltar).

Abbreviations

For Classical journals the abbreviations of *L'Annee Philologique* are used. Greek authors are abbreviated according to Liddell, Scott and Jones' *Greek Lexicon*. Latin authors are abbreviated according to the *Oxford Latin Dictionary*.

CHI = *Cambridge History of Iran*
CHIn = *Cambridge History of India*
EncIr = *Encyclopaedia Iranica*
FGrH = F. Jacoby, *Die Fragmente der griechischer Historiker*
J = *Jātaka*, ed. V. Fausbøll; tr. E.B. Cowell
JB = *Jaiminīya-Brāhmana of the Sāmaveda*, ed. R. Vira; German tr. W. Caland
MbH = *The Mahābhārata*, ed. V.S. Aukthankar et al.; tr. J.A.B. Van Buitenen
Manu = *The Laws of Manu*, ed. G. Gha; tr. G. Büher
NīlP = *Nīlamatapurāna:* ed. K. de Vreese; tr. V. Kumari
P = *The Ashtādyhāyi of Pānini*, ed. and tr. S.C. Vasu
R = *The Rāmāyana of Vālmīki*, tr. R. Goldman and S.I. Pollock
Rājat = *Rājataranginī of Kalhana*, ed. and tr. M.A. Stein
RVm = *Rig Veda*, ed. F. Müller; tr. W.D. O'Flaherty; Ger. tr. K.F. Geldner
SB = *Shatapatha-Brāhmana*, ed. A. Weber; tr. J. Eggeling
WOI = *The Wealth of India: A Dictionary of Indian Raw Materials and Industrial Products*, Delhi

Bibliography

Amigues, S. (2003) 'Pour la table du Grand Roi', *JS* 1, 3-59.

Amigues, S. (2005) 'Les animaux nommés skolex dans les "Indica" de Ctésias, FGrH 45 (46)', *RPh* 79, 7-15.

Anati, E. (1968) *Rock Art in Central Arabia* (2 vols), Bibliothèque du Museon 50, Institut Orientaliste Bibliothèque de l'Université Lovain.

André, J. (1955) 'Les noms latins de l'hellébore', *REL* 32, 174-82.

André, J. (1958) *Notes de lexicographie botanique grecque*, Paris.

André, J. and Filliozat, J. (1986) *L'Inde vue de Rome. Textes latins de l'antiquité relatifs à l'Inde*, Paris.

Arora, U.P. (1982) 'India vis-à-vis Egypt-Ethiopia in Classical accounts', *Graeco-Arabica* 1, 131-40.

Arora, U.P. (1991) *Graeco-Indica, India's Cultural Contects [sic] with the Greek World: in Memory of Demetrius Galanos (1760-1833), a Greek Sanskritist of Benares*, New Delhi.

Arora, U.P. (1996) *Greeks on India: Scylax to Aristoteles*, Isgars.

Auberger, J. (1991) *Ctesias: Histoires de l'Orient*, Paris.

Auboyer, J. (1965) *Daily Life in Ancient India, from approximately 200 BC to 700 AD*, tr. S.W. Taylor, New York.

Aujac, G. (1966) *Strabon et la sciene de son temps*, Paris.

Bähr, J.C.F. (1824) *Ctesiae Cnidii operum reliquiae*, Frankfurt.

Ball, V. (1883) 'The identification of the Pygmies, the Martikhora, the Griffins, and the Dikairon of Ktesias', *Indian Antiquary* 12, 234-5.

Ball, V. (1884a) 'A geologist's contribution to the history of ancient India. Early notices of metals and gems in India', *Indian Antiquary* 13, 228-48.

Ball, V. (1884b) 'The "Parebon" tree of Ktesias', *The Academy*, 280.

Ball, V. (1885) 'On the Identification of the Animals and the Plants of India which were known to early Greek Authors', *Indian Antiquary* 14, 274-87, 303-11, 334-41.

Banerjee, G.M. (1920) *Hellenism in Ancient India*, Calcutta.

Bartelink, G.J.M. (1972) 'Het fabeldier martichoras of mantichora', *Hermeneus* 43, 169-74, 225.

Becerra Romero, D. (2007) 'El *Díkairon* en la obra *Indika* de Ctesias de Cnido. Propuesta de identificación', *Emerita* 75, 255-72.

Benet, S. (1975) 'Early diffusion and folk uses of hemp', in *Cannabis and Culture*, ed. V. Rubin, The Hague, 39-49.

Benveniste, E. (1929) 'Le nom d'un animal Indien chez Élien', in *Donum Natalicium Schrijnen. Verzameling van opstellen door oud-leerlingen en bevriende vakgenooten opgedragen aan Mgr. Prof. Dr. Jos. Schrijnen bij Gelegenheid van zijn zestigsten verjaardag 3. Mei 1929*, ed. St W.J. Teeuwen, Nijmegen-Utrecht, 371-6.

Bigwood J.M. (1964) 'Ctesias of Cnidus', Diss. Harvard University.

Bigwood J.M. (1965) 'Ctesias of Cnidus', *HSPh* 70, 263-5.

Bigwood J.M. (1978) 'Ctesias as historian of the Persian Wars', *Phoenix* 32, 19-41.

Bigwood J.M. (1989) 'Ctesias' *Indica* and Photius', *Phoenix* 43, 302-16.

Bigwood J.M. (1993a) 'Aristotle and the elephant again', *AJP* 114, 537-55.

Bigwood J.M. (1993b) 'Ctesias' parrot', *CQ* 43, 321-7.

Bigwood J.M. (1995) 'Ctesias, his royal patrons and Indian swords', *JHS* 115, 135-40.

Binsfeld, W. (1956) *Grylloi*, Cologne.

Bisi, A.M. (1964) 'Il grifone nel' arte dell' Antico Irane e dei popoli delle steppe', *RSO* 39, 15-60.

Bisi, A.M. (1965) *Il grifone. Storia di un motivo iconografico nell'antico Oriente mediterraneo*, Rome.

Bolton, J.D.P. (1962) *Aristeas of Proconnesus*, Oxford.

Boucharlat, R. and Labrousse, A. (1979) 'Le palais d' Artaxerxès II sur la rive droite du Chaour à Suse', *CDAFI* 10, 19-154.

Braund, D. (2002) 'Indian traders at Phasis: neglected texts on ancient Georgia', in *Pont-Euxin et Commerce*, ed. M. Faudot et al., Paris, 287-95.

Briant, P. (1988) 'Le nomadisme du Grand Roi', *Iranica Antiqua* 23, 253-73.

Briant, P. (2002) *From Cyrus to Alexander: A History of the Persian Empire*, Winona Lake.

Briggs, G.W. (1931) 'The Indian rhinoceros as a sacred animal', *JAOS* 51, 276-82.

Brockington, J. (2003) 'The Sanskrit epics', in *The Blackwell Companion to Hinduism*, ed. G. Flood, Oxford, 116-28.

Brosius, M. (1996) *Women in Ancient Persia (559-331 BC)*, Oxford.

Brown T.S. (1955) 'The reliability of Megasthenes', *AJPh* 76, 28-33.

Brown T.S. (1978) 'Suggestions for a Vita of Ctesias of Cnidus', *Historia* 27 (1978) 1-19.

Bibliography

Calmeyer, P. (1989) 'Der "Apollon" des Dareios', *AMI* 22, 125-30.

Charpentier, J. (1911-1912) 'Beiträge zur alt- und mittelindischen Wortkunde', *IF* 29, 367-403.

Chattopadhyaya, A. (1967) 'A note on ancient Indian hunting dogs', *Indo-Asian Culture* 16, 231-34.

Chattopadhyaya, S. (1974) *The Achaemenids and India*, Delhi.

Dahlquist, A. (1996) *Megasthenes and Indian Religion: A Study in Motives and Types*, Delhi.

Dani, A.H. (1967) 'Report on the excavation of Balambhat settlement site', *Ancient Pakistan* 3, 235-88.

De Anna, L. (1998) *Thule: le fonti e le tradizioni*, Rimini.

Eastman, C.R. (1906) 'The real unicorn', *Science* XXIII, 195.

Eck, B. (1990) 'Sur la vie de Ctésias', *REG* 103, 409-34.

Edwards, M.L. 'Deaf and dumb in ancient Greece', in *The Disabilities Reader*, ed. J.L. Davis, CITY, 29-51.

Einhorn, J.W. (1976) *Spiritalis Unicornis. Das Einhorn als Bedeutungsträger in Literatur und Kunst des Mittelalters*, Munich.

Espelosín, F.J.G. (1994) 'Estrategias de veracidad en Ctesias de Cnido', *Polis* 6, 143-68.

Filliozat, J. (1981) 'La valeur des connaissances gréco-romaines sur l'Inde', *JS*, 97-135.

Flattery, D.S. and Schwartz, M. (1989) *Haoma and Harmaline: The Botanical Identity of the Indo-Iranian Sacred Hallucinogen 'Soma' and its Legacy in Religion, Language, and Middle Eastern Folklore*, Berkeley.

Frazer, J.G. (1920) *The Golden Bough: A Study in Magic and Religion*, 6 vols, New York.

Francfort, H.-P. (1978-1979) 'About the Shortughaï Sequence, from Mature Harappan to Late Bactrian: Bronze Age in Eastern Bactria (N.E. Afghanistan)', *Puratattva* 10, 91-4.

Francfort, H.-P. (1983) 'Excavations at Shortughaï in Northeast Afghanistan', *AJA* 87, 518-19.

Frisk, H. (1960-1972) *Griechisches Etymologisches Wörterbuch*, Heidelberg.

Funk, H. (forthcoming a) *Hyaena. On the Naming and Localisation of an Enigmatic Animal*.

Funk, H. (forthcoming b) 'How the ancient Krokottas evolved into the modern Spotted Hyena *Crocuta crocuta*'.

Fussman, G. (1985) 'La notion d'unité indienne dans l'antiquité. 1. Les auteurs grecs et latins', *Annuaire du Collège de France 1984-1985*, pp. 639-48.

Gardin, J.-C. (1997) *Prospections archéologiques en Bactriane Orientale (1974-1978)*, Paris.

Gera, D.L. (2003) *Ancient Greek Ideas on Speech, Language and Civilization*, Oxford.

Giannini, A. (1963) 'Studi sulla paradossografia greca, I. Da Omero a Callimaco: motivi e forme del meraviglioso', *RIL* 97, 247-66.

Gilmore, J. (1888) *The Fragments of the* Persika *of Ktesias*, London.

Girard, M.C. (1988) *Connaissance et méconnaissance de l'hellébore dans l'Antiquité*, Quebec.

Glover, T.R. 'Some curiosities of ancient warfare', *G&R* 19, 1-9.

Goldman, B. (1960) 'The Development of the Lion-Griffin', *AJA* 63, 319-28.

Goldman, R.P. (2005) *Rāmāyana: Book One: Boyhood, By Vālmīki*, New York.

Gotfredsen, L. (1999) *The Unicorn*, New York.

Goukowsky, P. (1972) 'Le roi Pôros, son éléphant et quelques autres (En marge de Diodore, XVII,88,6)', *BCH* 96, 473-502.

Grandjouan, C. (1961) *The Athenian Agora 6: Terracottas and Plastic Lamps*, Princeton.

Groves, C.P. (1974) *Horses, Asses, and Zebras in the Wild*, London.

Groves, C.P. and Mazák, V. (1967) 'On some taxonomic problems of Asiatic wild asses; with the description of a new subspecies (Perissodactyla; Equidae)', *Zeitschrift für Säugetierkunde* 32, 321-55.

Hansen, G.C. (1965) 'Ein unechtes Ktesiasfragment (F GrHist 588F63)', *Helikon* 5, 159-62.

Hasan, K.A. (1975) 'Social aspects of the use of cannabis in India', in *Cannabis and Culture*, ed. V. Rubin, The Hague, 235-46.

Henry, R. (1947) *Ctésias, la Perse, l'Inde, les sommaires de Photius*, Brussels.

Henry, R. (1959) *Photius: La Bibliothéque*, Paris.

Herrmann, A. (1920) 'Σαρδώνυξ ὄρος', *RE IA*, 2496.

Herrmann, A. (1923) 'Seres', *RE IIA*, 1678-83.

Herrmann, A. (1929) 'Skiapodes', *RE IIIA*, 517-18.

Hinüber, O. von (1985) *Arrian. Der Alexanderzug. Indische Geschichte*, Munich.

Holland, R. (1926) 'Zu den Indika des Ctesias', *Hermes* 235-7.

Holzberg, N. (2003) 'Novel-like works of extended prose fiction II', in *The Novel in the Ancient World*, ed. G. Schmeling, Leiden, 619-53.

Bibliography

Hornbostel, W. and Kropatscheck, W. (1980) *Aus Gräber und Heilitümern*, Hamburg.

Jacoby, F. (1923-) *Die Fragmente der griechischen Historiker*, Berlin.

Jacoby, F. (1922) 'Ktesias', *RE* XI, 2032-73.

James, R.M. (1887) 'Note on dikairon', *CR* 1, 24.

Janko, R. (2009) 'The Artemidorus Papyrus', *CR* 59, 403-10.

Janvier, Y. (1984) 'Rome et l'Orient lointain: le problème des Sères. Réexamen d'une question de géographie antique', *Ktema* 9, 261-303.

Jerdon, T.C. (1874) *The Mammals of India: A Natural History of all the Animals Known to Inhabit Continental India*, London.

Johnston, E.H. (1942) 'Ctesias on Indian manna', *Journal of the Royal Asiatic Society of Great Britain and Ireland*, 29-35.

Jouana, J. (1999) *Hippocrates*, tr. M.B. DeBevoise, Baltimore.

Kapparis, K. (2002) *Abortion in the Ancient World*, London.

Karttunen, K. (1981) 'The reliability of the *Indika* of Ctesias', *Studia Orientalia* 50, 105-7.

Karttunen, K. (1984) 'Κυνοκέφαλοι and κυναμολγοί in Classical ethnography', *Arctos* 18, 31-6.

Karttunen, K. (1985) 'A miraculous fountain in India', *Arctos* 19, 55-65.

Karttunen, K. (1987) 'The country of fabulous beasts and naked philosophers – India in classical and medieval literature', *Arctos* 21, 43-52.

Karttunen, K. (1989) *India in Early Greek Literature*, Helsinki.

Karttunen, K. (1991) 'The Indica of Ctesias and its criticism', in *Graeco-Indica, India's cultural contects* [*sic*] *with the Greek World: in Memory of Demetrius Galanos (1760-1833), a Greek Sanskritist of Benares*, New Delhi, 74-85.

Karttunen, K. (1996) 'Ctesias in transmission and tradition', *Topoi* 7, 635-46.

Karttunen, K. (1997a) *India and the Hellenistic World*, Helsinki.

Karttunen, K. (1997b) 'Greeks and Indian wisdom', in *Beyond Orientalism: The Work of Wilhelm Halbfass and its Impact on Indian and Cross-Cultural Studies*, ed. E. Franco and K. Preisendanz, Amsterdam, 117-22.

Karttunen, K. (2002) 'The ethnography of the fringes', in *Brill's Companion to Herodotus*, ed. E. Bakker, I. de Jong and H. van Wees, Leiden, 457-74.

Karttunen, K. (2008) 'Ctesias on falconry revisited', in *Intercultural Relations between South and Southwest Asia: Studies in Commemoration of E.C.L. During Caspers (1934-1996)*, ed. E. Olijdam and R.H. Spoor, Oxford, 358-60.

Kiessling, M. (1916) 'Hypobaros', *RE* 9, 329-32.

Kilmer, M.F. (1993) *Greek Erotica on Attic Red-figure Vases*, London.

Kirtley, B.F. (1963) 'The ear-sleepers: some permutations of a traveler's tale', *JAmFolklore* 76, 119-30.

Kollesch, J. (1989) 'Knidos als Zentrum der frühen wissenschaftlichen Medizin im alten Griechland', *Gesnerus* 46, 11-28.

König, F.W. (1972) *Die Persika des Ktesias von Knidos*, Graz.

Kumar, V. (1974) 'Social life in Ancient India as described in the Indika of Ktesias', *ABORI* 55, 239-42.

Lassen, C. (1874) *Indische Alterumskunde*, Leipzig.

Laufer, B. (1914) *Chinese Clay Figures, Part I: Prolegomena on the History of Defensive Armour*, Chicago.

Laufer, B. (1919) *Sino-Iranica*, Chicago.

Le Coq, A. (1914) 'Bemerkungen über Türkischen Falknerei', *Baessler-Archiv* 4, 1-13.

Lenfant, D. (1991) 'Milieu naturel et différences ethnique dans la pensée grecque classique', *Ktéma* 16, 111-22.

Lenfant, D. (1994) *Ctésias de Cnide. Edition, traduction et commentaire historique des témoignages et fragments*, Diss. Paris-IV-Sorbonne.

Lenfant, D. (1995) 'L'Inde de Ctésias: des sources aux représentations', *Topoi* 5, 309-36.

Lenfant, D. (1999) 'Monsters in Greek ethnography and society in the fifth and fourth centuries BCE', in *From Myth to Reason? Studies in the Development of Greek Thought*, ed. R. Buxton, Oxford 197-214.

Lenfant, D. (2004) *Ctésias de Cnide. La Perse, L'Inde, Autres Fragments*, Paris.

Lévi, S. (1904) 'The Kharoshtri writing and its cradle', *IA 33*, 79-84.

Lewis, D.M. (1987) 'The King's dinner (Polyaenus IV.3.32)', *Achaemenid History 2*, 89-91.

Lindegger, P. (1979) *Griechische und römische Quellen zum peripheren Tibet. Teil I. Frühe Zeugnisse bis Herodot (Der fernere skythische Nordosten)*, Zurich.

Lindegger, P. (1982) *Griechische und römische Quellen zum peripheren Tibet. Teil II. Überlieferungen von Herodot bis zu den Alexanderhistorikern (Die nordösten Grenzregionen Indiens)*, Zurich.

Lindner, K. (1973) *Beiträge zu Vogelfang und Falknerei in Altertum*, Berlin.

Lonie, I.M. (1978) 'Cos versus Cnidus and the historians', *HS* 16, 42-75, 77-92.

Loud, G. (1936) *Khorsabad Part I. Excavations in the Palace and at the City Gate*, Chicago.

Bibliography

Maas, P. (1924) 'Ein Exzerpt aus Ktesias Ινδικά bei Michel Psellos', *Zeitschrift für vergleichende Sprachforschung aus dem Gebeite der indogermanischen Sprache*, 52, 303-6.

Malte-Brun (1819) 'Mémoire sur l'Inde Septentrionale d'Hérodote et de Ctésias comparée au Petit-Tibet des modernes', *Nouvelles Annales des Voyages* 2, 307-83.

Manchester, K. (1992) 'Leprosy: the origin and development of the disease in antiquity', in *Maladie et maladies: histoire et conceptualisation: mélanges en l'honneur de Mirko Grmek*, ed. D. Gourevitch, Geneva, 31-49.

Marquart, J. (1913) *Die Benin-Sammlung des Reichsmuseums für Völkerkunde in Leiden*, Leiden.

McCrindle, J.W. (1881) 'Ancient India as described by Ktesias', *Indian Antiquary* X, 296-323.

MacDonald, G. (1936) 'Thule', *RE VI A*, col. 627-30.

Matchett, F. (2003) 'The Purānas', in *The Blackwell Companion to Hinduism*, ed. G. Flood, Oxford, 129-43.

Momigliano, A. (1982) 'Gli *Indika* di Megastene', *Annali della Scuola Normale Superiore di Pisa*, Serie 3, vol. 12.1, pp. 71-49.

Monier-Williams, M. (1976) *A Sanskrit-English Dictionary: Etymologically and Philologically Arranged With Special Reference to Cognate Indo-European Languages*, New Delhi.

Müller, C. (1844) *Ctesiae Cnidii et Chronographorum Castoris, Eratosthenes, etc. Fragmenta*, Paris.

Mund-Dopchie, M. and Vanbaelen, S. (1989) 'L'Inde dans l'imaginaire grec', *Etudes Classiques* 57, 209-26.

Olmstead, A.T. (1948) *History of the Persian Empire*, Chicago.

Oppenheim, A.L. (1985) 'The Babylonian evidence of Achaemenian rule in Mesopotamia', *CHI 2*, 529-87.

Page, J.A. (1930) 'Bulandi Bagh, near Patna', in *Archaeological Survey of India, Annual Report for 1926-1927*, ed. J. Marshall, 135-40.

Panaino, A. (2001) 'Between Mesopotamia and India: some remarks about the unicorn cycle in Iran', in *Mythology and Mythologies: Methodological Approaches to Intercultural Influences*, ed. R.M. Whiting, Helsinki, 149-79.

Parker, G. (2008) *The Making of Roman India*, Cambridge.

Platt, A. (1909) 'On the Indian dog', *CQ 3*, 241-3.

Puskás, I. and Kádár, Z. (1980) 'Satyrs in India', *ACUSD 16*, 9-17.

Reese, W. (1914) *Die griechischen Nachrichten über Indien bis zum Feldzuge Alexanders des Grossen*, Leipzig.

Rettig, H.C.M. (1827) *Ctesiae Cnidii vita cum appendice de libris quos Ctesias compuisse fertut*, Leipzig.

Riddle, J.M. (1992) *Contraception and Abortion from the Ancient World to the Renaissance*, Cambridge.

Riese, A. (1878) *Geographi Latini Minores*, Heilbronn.

Robertson, M. (1979) 'A muffled dancer and others', in *Studies in Honour of Arthur Dale Trendall*, ed. A. Cambitoglou, Sydney.

Romm, J.S. (1989) 'Aristotle's elephant and the myth of Alexander's scientific patronage', *AJP* 110, 566-75.

Romm, J.S. (1992) *The Edges of the Earth in Ancient Thought: Geography, Exploration, and Fiction*, Princeton.

Root, M.C. (1979) *The King and Kingship in Achaemenid Art: Essays on the Creation of an Iconography of Empire*, Leiden.

Rougemont, G. (1977) *Corpus des inscriptions de Delphes, I: Lois sacrées et règlements religieux*, Paris.

Sachse, J. (1982) 'Le mythe des Sila, fleuve indien (Mégasthène FGrHist 715, F. 10)', *Eos 70*, 237-41.

Salonen, A. (1973) *Vögel und Vogelfang im alten Mesopotamien*, Helsinki.

Sariandi, V. (1988) 'Cult symbolism of Bactrian and Margiana amulets', in *Orientalia Iosephi Tucci memoriae dictata*, ed. G. Gnoli and L. Lanciotti, Rome, 1281-94.

Sariandi, V. (1998) *Myths of Ancient Bactria and Margiana on its Seals and Amulets*, Moscow.

Sbordone, F. (1936) *Physiologus*, Milan.

Schepens, G. and Delcroix, K. (1996) 'Ancient paradoxography: origin, evolution, production and reception', in *La letteratura di consumo nel mundo Greco Latino,* ed. O. Pecere and A. Stramaglia, Cassino, 374-460.

Schmidt, E.F. (1970) *Persepolis III: The Royal Tombs and Other Monuments*, Chicago.

Schmidt, H.P. (1980) 'The Sēnmurw. Of birds and dogs and bats', *Persica 9*, 1-85.

Schmitt, R. (2006) *Iranische Anthroponyme in den Erhaltenen Resten von Ktesias' Werk*, Vienna.

Schwanbeck, E.A. (1856) *Megasthenis Indica. Feagmenta colegit, commentationem et indicices addidit*, Bonn.

Scullard, H.H. (1974) *The Elephant in the Greek and Roman World*, Cambridge.

Sergent, B. (1998) 'Les Sères sont les soi-disant "Tokhariens", c'est-à-dire les authentiques Arsi-Kuci', *DHA* 24, 7-40.

Bibliography

Shafer, R. (1964) 'Unmasking Ktesias' dogheaded people', *Historia* 13, 499-503.

Shapiro, H.A. (1984) 'Notes on Greek dwarfs', *AJA* 88, 391-2.

Shepard, O. (1930) *The Lore of the Unicorn*, London.

Shrimpton, G.S. (1991) *Theopompus the Historian*, Montreal.

Schulze, W. (1924) Addendum to Maas (1924).

Schwartz, J. (1986) 'De quelques mentions antiques des Sères', *Ktema* 11, 289-90.

Smyth, H.W. (1956) *Greek Grammar*, Cambridge.

Solomou, S. (2007) *The* Indica *of Ctesias of Cnidus: Te*xt *(incl. MSS. Monacensis gr. 287 and Oxoniensis, Holkham gr. 110), Translation and Commentary*, Diss. University College London.

Steier, A. (1924) 'Hyäene', *RE Suppl. IV*, col. 761-8.

Steier, A. (1938) 'Pfeffer', *RE XIX*, col. 1421-5.

Stoneman, R. (2008) *Alexander the Great: A Life in Legend*, New Haven.

Stronach, D. (1987) 'Apadāna', *Encyclopaedia Iranica Online*, available at www.iranica.com.

Stronk, J.P. (2007) 'Ctesias of Cnidus, a reappraisal', *Mnemosyne* 60, 25-58.

Thapar, V. (1997) *Land of the Tiger: A Natural History of the Indian Subcontinent*, Berkeley.

Trotter, S. (1908) 'Concerning the real unicorn', *Science* 28, 608-9.

Tuplin, C.J. (2004) 'Doctoring the Persians: Ctesias of Cnidus physician and historian', *Klio* 86, 305-47.

Vallat, F. (1979) 'Les inscriptions du palais d'Artaxerxès II sur la rive droite du Chaour', *CDAFI* 10, 145-54.

Vallat, F. (1989) 'Le palais d'Artaxerxès II à Babylone', *NAPR* 2, 3-6.

Veltheim, A.F. Graf von, (1797) *Etwas über die Onyxgebirge des Ctesias und den Handel der Alten nach Ost-Indien*, Helmstädt.

Vögele, H.H. (1931) *Die Falknerei. Eine ethnographische Darstellung*, Neudamm.

Vogel, J.P., (1926) *Indian Serpent-Lore*, Delhi.

Vogelsang, W.J., (1992) *The Rise and Organization of the Achaemenid Empire*, Leiden.

Wecker, O. (1925) 'κυνοκέφαλοι', *RE* XII, col. 25-6.

Westrem, S.D. (2001) *The Hereford Map*, Turnhout.

Wheeler, J.T. (1874) *The History of India From the Earliest Times*, vol. III, London.

White, D. (1991) *Myths of the Dog-man*, Chicago.

Whitfield, S. and Sims-Williams, U. (2004) *The Silk Road: Trade, Travel, War, and Faith*, Chicago.

Wilson, H.H. (1836) 'Notes on the *Indica* of Ctesias', *Transactions of the Ashmolean Society* 1, 5-80.

Wittkower, R. (1942) 'Marvels of the East: a study in the history of monsters', *Journal of the Warburg and Courtauld Institutes* 5, 159-97.

Witzel, M. (2003) 'Vedas and Upanishads', in *The Blackwell Companion to Hinduism*, ed. G. Flood, Oxford, 68-98.

Young, W.J. (1972) 'The fabulous gold of the Pactolus Valley', *Bulletin: Museum of Fine Arts, Boston* 70, 5-13.

Ziegler, K. (1949) 'Παραδοξόγραφοι', *RE* XVIII, col. 1137-66.

Index Locorum

References to the pages and notes of this book are in bold type.

General Index

Page numbers in bold refer to the text of the translation.